As you read this may you be reminded of Gods great love for you — Eph 3:16-19

Carol Nee

As you read this
now you be persuaded
of Gods great love
for you.
Feb 24th 19

FAREWELL, MY FREE BIRD

A mother's story of her daughter's life in the dark world of drugs and prostitution . . . and the phone call that changed their family forever.

Carol Noe

authorHOUSE®

AuthorHouse™
1663 Liberty Drive
Bloomington, IN 47403
www.authorhouse.com
Phone: 1-800-839-8640

© 2011 by Carol Noe. All rights reserved.

No part of this book may be reproduced, stored in a retrieval system, or transmitted by any means without the written permission of the author.

First published by AuthorHouse   09/27/2011

ISBN: 978-1-4670-3686-3 (sc)
ISBN: 978-1-4670-3685-6 (hc)
ISBN: 978-1-4670-3684-9 (ebk)

Library of Congress Control Number: 2011916507

Printed in the United States of America

Any people depicted in stock imagery provided by Thinkstock are models, and such images are being used for illustrative purposes only.
Certain stock imagery © Thinkstock.

This book is printed on acid-free paper.

Because of the dynamic nature of the Internet, any web addresses or links contained in this book may have changed since publication and may no longer be valid. The views expressed in this work are solely those of the author and do not necessarily reflect the views of the publisher, and the publisher hereby disclaims any responsibility for them.

DEDICATION

This book is dedicated with love to my husband, and lifelong companion, Keith, and to our sons, Carl, Travis and Jason. Without your support, and your prayers and constant encouragement, this book would not have been possible.

TABLE OF CONTENTS

Foreword vii
Acknowledgments ix
Introduction xi

1. No One Dares To Die Before His Time 1
2. Memories 5
3. So Much Pain Within 15
4. Can This Be Reality? 23
5. Why Can't The World Let Me Be? 33
6. I Try To Fit In But I Can't 47
7. I Just Wish I Was Free 59
8. I Do As I Please 67
9. Mixed Feelings 73
10. Never Again 83
11. Crying In The Middle Of The Night 93
12. I Just Want To Be Free To Be Me 103
13. I Am The Lonely In Your Heart 111
14. I Really Don't Want To Die 125
15. The Day Is New 139
16. A Glimpse Of My God 149
17. Rise Up And Spread Your Wings 157
18. Reaching Out Together 167
19. Miracles And Revelations 177
20. Healing For The Family Justice For Angela 187
21. To God Be The Glory 197

Epilogue 209

FOREWORD

I would like to commend Carol for telling her story like it really was—and really is. She doesn't pull any punches when she exposes her life and her heart for all of us to see . . . and see we must. We are surrounded by heart-wrenching stories every time we watch the news and forget that these are real people whose lives will never be the same.

As a former paramedic, now serving as a pastor and emergency services chaplain, I have been exposed to so much death, grief and loss over the years. What I have learned is this—tragic loss and pain doesn't need to be the end of anyone's story.

Farewell, My Free Bird is a raw, yet tender story told through the deep honesty and transparency of a mother's love. It was not easy to live or easy to tell. Only someone who has survived the pain and discovered the purpose and healing of Jesus Christ can write like this. This is not another "woe-is-me" story but rather a "yes-this-happened-to-us, but-look-what-God-has-done" account. In a simple straightforward style, Carol helps us see THE truth she discovered that still sets people free.

I invite you to relive the compelling journey of, *Farewell, My Free Bird;* and, perhaps, you too will be filled with new hope as you come face-to-face with the healing power of God's love and forgiveness.

Pastor Paul Taylor
Author of *Too Many Lovers*

ACKNOWLEDGMENTS

My special thanks to the following people:

My husband, Keith, who patiently and unselfishly stood by me and supported me in every way, through the many years it took for me to write the book.

Our sons, Carl, Jason, and Travis, for their willingness and courage to let me publicly share our lives in the hope that someone else could be helped by Angela's story. I am very proud of the men you have become.

Denise LaRosh for the many hours you spent reading the manuscript. Your editorial advice and assistance was invaluable.

Ron Lang, Scott Moore, Beverly Gunn, and Marla Davis for your input and for proof reading the manuscript before it was submitted for publication.

Gary Blinn and Dawn Mundy for editing the manuscript in the early period of writing this book.

Paul and Barb Taylor for your encouragement and your help as I began the process of submitting the manuscript to the publisher.

Rhonda Gibler for your time and professional help formatting the pictures for the book.

I am indebted to many other friends and family who have encouraged me and prayed for the completion of the book. If I were to attempt to name each one of you, I would run the risk of leaving out someone of importance. You know who you are. I want you to know I have been blessed by your help, your prayers, and your support.

Most of all, I thank God for His direction and for His grace that enabled me to write Angela's story. It is because of His faithfulness to Angela and to our family that I have a story to tell.

INTRODUCTION

As I write the story of my daughter, Angela, and her life that was filled with turmoil before her tragic murder, I pray that others will see God's faithfulness and His miracles as He brought our family peace even in the midst of our deepest pain.

Angela's story of her struggles with alcohol, drugs, and eventually prostitution is a painful story to tell, but I tell it because I believe it can bring healing and hope for someone else.

The phone call from the detective telling us that our nineteen-year-old daughter, Angela, had been shot and then stabbed to death was a nightmare come true. As we made plans for the funeral, my husband, Keith, our three sons, Carl, Travis, and Jason, and I were all in shock. That first night after the phone call from the detective, my heart was full of unbearable pain. I asked God . . . *Is she with you? I have to know.* In the days that followed, God answered that question and many others that we as a family had about Angela's life and death.

Angela was a sanguine at heart. She loved people and loved to do things for others just to make them happy. Wherever she went, she was surrounded by friends. As she neared her teenage years, we were alarmed as alcohol and drugs became an important part of her life. Eventually, Angela was deeply involved in a life of prostitution. Angela had a strong desire to be free to do what she wanted to do. She would tell me, "Mom, I want to be a *free bird!*" It didn't take long before those who loved her realized that her individual search for freedom was destroying her.

As I tell Angela's story, it is important to know that this is not a story of the *'perfect'* family who had a rebellious child. During the years Angela was addicted to alcohol and drugs, her dad remained loyal to his job and family, but he struggled with his own alcohol addiction. When Angela was sixteen, Keith made a significant decision to seek help and stopped drinking. We continue to thank God for this miracle.

When the children were very young, I became a Christian by accepting the Lord Jesus Christ. In my new-found faith I mistakenly thought it was up to me to live my life in such a way to earn God's love and approval. I set out in my own efforts to be the perfect Christian and have the perfect children. Looking back, I see that this also contributed to our family tensions. As I grew in my faith and experienced God's unconditional love and His wonderful grace, I realized that trying to be perfect for God was not only impossible, but that God did not expect me or my children to be perfect. Instead of my trying to perform and live *for* God, I learned that He wanted me to trust Him and allow Him to live His life *through* me. He continues to teach me more about His grace every day.

Our family has experienced some very good and some very difficult times, but always God has been faithful to each one of us. Our sons now have families of their own, and we are deeply blessed by our ten grandchildren who bring us unspeakable joy.

God challenged us to forgive and to pray for the man that murdered Angela. At first, I was offended that He would even ask such a thing. Even though we despised this man, in obedience to God, my husband and I prayed for him. We discovered that praying for Angela's murderer was significant in our healing process. We also began praying for the people involved in Angela's life at the time of her death. These were the witnesses for the murder trial that we would meet several years after Angela's death. God used one of the witnesses to answer a question I had been asking Him for years: *God, why was Angela's life so bizarre?* God used this witness to reveal to us that Angela had suffered other traumatic experiences in her teenage years that, until her murder trial, we had not been aware of.

Months before Angela was murdered, she and I had talked about writing a book about her life together. After her death, I sadly realized that this would never happen. Then, one afternoon, after she was gone, while I was going through the few possessions Angela had left, I was surprised to find a book of poems Angela had written. She had signed each poem, "FREE BIRD." In each of her hand-written poems, she expresses with great emotion what it was like for her during her teenage years. She wrote these poems up to the time she was murdered. I felt as though I had found a treasure.

When I began writing *Farewell, My Free Bird*, I knew Angela's poetry was meant to be a part of her story. I have included one of her poems at the end of most chapters. Also, with a few exceptions, the chapter titles are lines from her poems.

So, Angela and I wrote her story together after all. By leading me to her book of poetry, God provided the way.

(The New International Version of the Bible is used for all Scripture references unless otherwise noted.)

For various reasons, some of the names have been changed in this book.

CHAPTER ONE

NO ONE DARES TO DIE BEFORE HIS TIME

> *"Even though I walk through the valley of the shadow of death, I will fear no evil for you are with me." (Psalm 23:4)*

Afternoon, April 28, 1987:

"This is Detective Burns from the San Francisco Police Department. May I ask who I'm talking to?"

"This is Carol Noe."

"Do you have a daughter, Angela?"

"Yes, I do."

Angela lived with her friends in Oakland, California. This wouldn't be the first time a call from a police department had jolted and unnerved me. I wondered what kind of trouble Angela was in now. Anything I imagined could not have been as devastating as what he told me next.

"We have a homicide. We've fingerprinted the victim and she's been identified as your daughter, Angela Noe."

Angela? Victim? Homicide? No, this couldn't be true! Angela had been home only two weeks before on her nineteenth birthday. I had just talked with her on the phone a few days before.

"How can you be sure it's her?" I asked. This had to be a horrible mistake.

"Your daughter came in as 'Jane Doe' yesterday. She was fingerprinted and identified as Angela Noe. She's 5'9", brown hair, blue eyes, and has an appendix scar on her stomach."

A cold chill washed over me. Angela was four years old when we first admitted her to the hospital with ruptured appendicitis. But, a lot of girls have appendix scars.

The detective continued, "She has a tattoo on her left shoulder that says '*Free Bird.*'"

My safe denial was smashed to pieces. As a young teenager Angela came home one day and proudly showed me her tattoo. To her it was a mark of freedom and independence. She told me, "Mom, I want to be like a free bird!"

Stunned and shaking, I listened as the detective continued. "Your daughter has multiple gunshot and stab wounds. A man was walking his dog at the Lincoln Park Golf Course early yesterday morning and found her body."

My mind couldn't process any more. I wanted him to stop talking. Different thoughts fought for my attention. One screamed *she's dead!* The other pleaded *No, please this can't be true.* But, this *was* a nightmare come true.

I was numb when I hung up the phone. A hand rested on my shoulder. It was my thirteen year old son, Jason. He saw my tears and had heard enough of the conversation to know something was wrong. I looked into his questioning young face. How could I say these crushing words to him, words that were foreign to me?

"Mom? What happened?"

As tenderly as I could, I told my son that his sister was dead.

"Angela?" I watched him as he tried to comprehend what he had heard. We both were in shock and disbelief. There were no more words to say. We could only hold each other and cry. I had to let Keith know. My husband was a Los Angeles motorcycle police officer and hard to reach by phone. I called Su, my pastor's wife and my close friend.

"Su, Angela's been murdered! I need you to call Keith at work and tell him to call home."

"Oh Carol! I'll call Keith. Shawn and I will be there as soon as we can."

Within minutes, I met Su and Shawn at the door. I wept in their arms as I told them what happened.

Just then the phone rang. It was Keith calling from the police station.

"Carol, they said it was an emergency. What's going on?"

The words wouldn't come.

"Carol, what's wrong?"

"It's Angela. She's been murdered."

"Oh, God! No! I'm leaving for home right now."

"Please be careful."

Shawn and Jason left to get our seventeen-year old son, Travis, from work. He had just left the house minutes before the phone call from the detective.

Our twenty-one year old son, Carl, was a marine who was stationed in Yuma, Arizona. I wished I could have held him and comforted him when I spoke those devastating words to him on the phone.

"Carl, Angela's dead. She's been murdered."

There was silence.

Then he spoke. "Mom, I'll get permission to come home. I'll be there as soon as I can. My motorcycle is running good and . . ."

"Carl, get an airplane flight. We'll arrange for you to be picked up at the airport."

It was so important to me that everyone remain safe. Then the front door opened. It was Keith and a fellow police officer who had driven him home. Keith came toward me. We held each other trying to comprehend what had happened and draw strength from each other in the midst of the confusion and the pain we were feeling.

Soon the house was filled with family and friends.

Keith called the San Francisco Police Department to get more information and talked to Detective Burns. Yes, Angela had been murdered. Yes, she had been shot and stabbed. Yes, she was dead.

Later that night when everyone had left and we were alone with our three sons, we joined hands and asked God for His grace and strength to be able to face what was ahead. Painfully aware that Angela was missing, Keith spoke what we were all thinking. "From now on, it's just the five of us."

Our little girl was really gone.

> *It seems today that no one cares for really living,*
> *No one dares to die before his time to go.*
> *Though no one cares just when his time to go will be,*
> *Or where it finds him,*
> *He knows that death will strike or hit,*
> *Sometimes when he least expects.*
> *Angela, FREE BIRD*

(Poems written by Angela from her 'Book of Poems')

Chapter Two

MEMORIES

> *"For you created my inmost being; you knit me together in my mother's womb. I praise you because I am fearfully and wonderfully made." (Psalm 139:13-14)*

My mind was spinning when I laid my head on the pillow that night. It was the first time since the news of Angela's murder that Keith and I had a chance to be alone with our thoughts. Keith held me as I wept, clutching the pillow to my chest, trying to relieve the pain of my empty aching arms, realizing I would never hold my daughter again.

"Keith, this has to be a bad dream."

"I know," he answered.

My hand reached for a tissue, but stopped as I touched the wooden box Angela had made. My fingers felt the letters she had painted, '*Moms Tissue Box.*'

Sleep wouldn't come. Tormenting thoughts filled my mind with the horrors Angela must have gone through the night she was murdered. She was 5'9", slender, but strong and feisty. No one could hurt her without a struggle. She often appeared bold, but I knew the scared little girl under the tough veneer.

I wondered how long before her death she realized she was going to be killed. Did she know when she was driven to the deserted golf course? What was she feeling? A long distance shot had hit her in the back of her head, and the heel of her shoe had broken from fighting with or running from her attacker. What terror she must have felt as she ran screaming for her life. What was going through her mind when the bullets hit her body and she heard her murderer run closer to her? How desperate and alone she must have felt when he kept shooting and stabbing her, when she realized no one was responding to her cries for help. How long did she lie on the ground still alive? How much pain did she feel? What were her last thoughts as her life ebbed away? Did she call out for me? Why couldn't I have been there to help her, to hold her in my arms, to comfort her, to tell her that I loved her? Every time I closed my eyes, her screams haunted me.

Lord, help me! No one can live with this much pain!

I had to force my thoughts elsewhere. April 8th, 1968, the night Angela was born. Keith drove me to the hospital. After being checked in and given a room, Keith and I were timing my contractions when the hospital room started shaking. We were having an earthquake! The earthquake stopped, but my contractions intensified. This baby was coming soon.

Keith and I could hardly contain ourselves when the doctor announced, "It's a girl!"

"She's a big one too," he said. Angela weighed in at 9 lbs., 10½ oz. When the nurse lifted Angela up for me to see, I saw the most beautiful baby girl. My heart melted when they laid her next to me. Keith and I studied her perfectly formed body, her small fingers and toes, her curly dark hair, and her tiny round face. Life seemed perfect for us at that moment.

The day we brought Angela home, Carl ran toward me to wrap his little arms around my neck. He hadn't liked the idea of my leaving him to go to the hospital, but he gave his consent when we promised to return with a new baby brother or sister. He sat next to me on the sofa as I introduced him to his sister.

"Carl, this is Angela, your baby sister."

His eyes were taking in the wonder of it all. Carefully, he touched Angela's face and smiled. Then after a few minutes of taking it all in, he ran off to play.

Angela was a delightful baby. She eagerly nursed in my arms while I held her close to me. I was so thankful for this precious gift.

She slept peacefully between feedings. When I laid her down in her bassinet, her tiny thumb always found its way to her mouth. She seemed content and happy. She grew strong and sturdy. Her cute and charming ways made it easy for us to enjoy her. Once Angela could walk, she kept busy from the time she got up in the morning until the time she'd put her tired head on the pillow and fall asleep at night.

Angela was sixteen months old when Travis was born. She thought it was great fun to have a new baby in the house and she wanted to be mommy's helper. One morning, she ran into the kitchen to tell me, "Mommy, the baby's crying, hurry!"

"I'll be there in a moment."

She ran back to the bedroom and I could hear her reassuring Travis, "Mommy's coming. Just wait, Travis." Her reassuring words didn't stop his crying. "Travis, I *told* you it's all right." I heard one last exasperated, *"Travis!"* from Angela. Then, it was quiet. That's when I decided I'd better check on them both. Angela was coming down the hallway with Travis in her arms, barely hanging on to him, his tiny legs dragging on the floor.

"Mommy, he couldn't wait."

I spoke calmly, not wanting to alarm her, "Angela, stop right there. I'll come and get him from you." She was so proud she had rescued him; but agreed, after our talk, that only Mom or Dad could take him out of his bassinet.

Keith was working long hours, and being a young mother with small children, I felt discontented with just being at home. I joined a women's weekly Bible study. The first morning that I drove to the church, I wondered how I would ever get all three children from the car into the church building and to their classes. Carl, at the age of four, was a live-wire who constantly needed close supervision. Angela was two years old, and Travis was six months old. I took Carl by one hand, instructing Angela to hold his hand, and with my other hand I maneuvered Travis into his infant seat and tried to lead us in the direction of the church. Fortunately, a sympathetic, older lady helped me find the classes for the children. Angela started crying as soon as she realized I was leaving, but it didn't take her long to quiet down when the nursery worker pulled out a box of graham crackers. After the Bible study, I picked up the children. They had a great time and were excited to show me the crafts they had made. The car was filled with singing on the way home as they sang the new songs they had learned.

"Jesus Loves Me" became one of Angela's favorite songs. As I reminisced, I could almost hear Angela singing. *"Jesus loves me this I know, for the Bible tells me so . . . Little ones to Him belong. We are weak but He is strong."* She would always stress the last two lines, raising her voice and shouting out *"Yes, Jesus loves me. Yes, Jesus loves me. Yes, Jesus loves me 'cause the Bible tells me so!"*

We continued going to the weekly Bible study for several years. The kids loved it, and I was learning a lot about God and His Word. It was during this time I prayed to receive Jesus Christ into my life as my Lord and Savior.

Each night when I tucked Angela in we'd talk about her day, any fears she might have, what new toys she wanted, or whom she would play with the next day. Then, we'd close with a prayer. I still can remember those precious times when she would pray, "God bless our family and keep us safe. I pray that everyone in the whole world will know about You and accept You into their hearts. Amen." Then, I'd pray while she listened, thanking God for her and for His many blessings. I'd kiss her goodnight, and before she fell asleep her little thumb would still find its way to her mouth.

She enjoyed being with Keith and followed him around the house. One morning, while Keith was shaving, Angela stood in awe watching everything he did. Then Keith told her she had to leave while he took his shower. She walked out; he shut the door behind her. Immediately, she started hollering. "Daddy, open the door!" While he took his shower, he heard her insistent crying. "Open the door!"

"Angela, I'll be done in a few minutes. Go and play."

But she didn't leave. Several minutes passed before the crying and the pounding on the door stopped. Relieved, Keith finished his shower. When he opened the door a piece of Angela's nightgown dropped to the floor at his feet. He realized he had closed the door on part of her nightgown. Her cries were out of her desperation to be set free. Picking up the torn piece of material, he found Angela in her room playing with her dolls. He chuckled at the big gaping hole in her nightgown. She turned and saw him. "Daddy, why didn't you open the door? I was stuck."

He quickly apologized and she quickly forgave him.

As she neared the age of five, she constantly talked about going to school just like her big brother, Carl. She wanted to do *pretend* homework and would give it to me to grade. Finally, her big day came.

I smiled as I went into her room and saw her lying in bed with her thumb in her mouth, and pink rollers in her hair.

"Angela, wake up. This is your big day." She sat up with a start. Her little legs dropped onto the hardwood floor. Still groggy, she followed me into the kitchen for breakfast. It took some time to comb her hair just the way she liked it. She put her pretty pink dress on that we were saving for this special day and rushed into the kitchen to get her new lunch pail.

As we walked together to the school that was at the end of our block she asked, "Do you think anyone will want to be my friend?"

She looked to me for reassurance. She was so young, so vulnerable. I prayed this would be a good day for her and that God would let her find a special friend.

As we stood outside the kindergarten classroom, Angela and another little girl started talking to each other. As the teachers lined up the children to go inside, the two girls stood together, and Angela happily waved goodbye.

Angela loved school. Each day she would come home excited about the things she was learning and about her many new friends. But one day she returned home with tears falling from her face.

"Mom, there's this boy at school. He's mean. He pushed me down, and look what he did!" Her dress was muddy and her special lunch pail was dented. "He pushed me in the mud right in front of everyone." She was humiliated and never wanted to go back to school. But, the next morning she left for school with a smile on her face and with the knowledge that not everyone would always be kind to her.

Jason, our fourth child, was born in October a few months after Angela started kindergarten. Several weeks before Jason was to be born, Angela and I spent an afternoon baking and decorating a cake. We put it in the freezer for that special day when her brother would be brought home. That special day came and when Carl, Angela, and Travis met their new little brother, Jason, for the first time, our family celebrated his 'birth' day with our cake. Keith and I had three gifts wrapped and ready for each of the kids from Jason. Angela spent lots of time singing to Jason and telling him stories while he lay in his bassinet.

Her life now was also filled with the challenges of school. At the first Parent-Teacher conference, the teacher told me that Angela was demanding more attention than she could give her. I purposed to spend more time with her. As the years went by, the need for extra attention was something I would hear more than once from teachers as she progressed through school.

Angela excelled in memorization, but subjects like Science and Math overwhelmed her. Many nights she cried and argued with me out of frustration while we struggled with her homework. It was difficult for her to concentrate on her work at school.

One evening, after all four of the kids had been bathed, brushed their teeth, finished their homework and had a goodnight kiss, I walked to my bedroom and fell onto the bed exhausted. The phone rang. It was Angela's teacher.

"I'm having problems with Angela. She doesn't always listen when I give instructions, and she likes to visit with her friends during class. I tried moving her desk away from her friends, but that didn't keep her from distracting the other students around her."

I prayed, asking God to give me wisdom to know what to do. As I was praying, a thought came to me that I believed was from God. *"Prayer will make the difference!"* It left a strong impression on me. I felt comforted and thanked God for what I believed was His answer. I began praying for my children consistently, knowing more than ever how important it would be.

As our family outgrew our little home, we moved into a spacious two-story house. What an exciting day it was! The first thing the children did was to find their bedrooms, and the boys needed to be reminded not to slide down the banister on the staircase. That same day was Angela's eighth birthday, so we celebrated a double blessing.

We discovered there was another new family in the neighborhood that had moved in the week before us. Their daughter, Paula, nine years old, was looking for a friend. Angela and Paula met and immediately established a friendship that would last for years. They would spend hours sharing their little girl secrets, and running back and forth from Paula's house to ours. Full and busy years passed by all too quickly as our four children grew.

By the time she was thirteen, Angela was attractive and outgoing. Sometimes she would share her concerns with me about feelings of inferiority. She didn't believe she was pretty. She worried about being too tall. Yet she carried herself with confidence that concealed her uneasiness about herself. Angela had a driving intensity and she wanted to experience everything in life . . . now! We joked about her being thirteen going on forty. However, it ceased to be humorous when Angela began boldly defying those in authority.

I was noticing increasing mood swings and changes in her attitude at home. I tried to find ways to show her I cared. One afternoon, I spread a blanket out on the den floor and took every movable plant from inside and outside of the house, placing them around the blanket. I set a bud vase with a single rose in the center. Angela always loved plants and flowers. I closed the door to the den, hurried to the kitchen, mixed lemonade, and tore open a bag of cookies. Just as I finished, Angela walked into the house carrying her school books.

"Angela, do you want to go on a picnic with me?"

She gave me a strange look. "A picnic now?"

I nodded.

"Where?" She asked.

"It's a surprise. Do you want to go?"

"I guess."

"You go upstairs and change. I'll get the food ready."

It didn't take her long before she was downstairs ready to go. I placed the drinks and cookies in a basket and handed it to her.

"Alright. Let's go." I headed toward the den.

"Where are you going? The car is out this way."

"Come on. You'll see."

I opened the den door, "Ta Da!"

Her eyes lit up. She was speechless. She laughed.

"This is great. It looks like a real park. This is silly," she said, "but I like it." Several times I saw her studying our transformed den.

We sat on the blanket, eating our cookies and drinking lemonade, talking like we used to, and discussing her day at school.

Sadly, those special times became fewer. Her rebellion escalated. She rejected our love and our discipline, and began making choices that were not good for her. Her teenage years became filled with turmoil and pain for all of us.

As I lay in bed the night of that fateful phone call, reminiscing about Angela, and trying to comprehend the bitter reality that Angela had been murdered, a noise interrupted my thoughts. I noticed a light shining through my bedroom door. I glanced at the clock. It was 1 a.m. I got out of bed and went downstairs. Travis was at the kitchen table working on his homework.

"Can't sleep, Travis?"
"No."
"Neither can I."
"I want to go to school tomorrow," he said.
"You don't have to."
"I know. But I want to."
Carl's bedroom door was open. "Where's Carl?"
"He couldn't sleep either. He went to the coffee shop."

I looked at Travis' tired face. He was trying so hard not to feel the pain. I hugged him. "I love you. Try to get some sleep. Goodnight."

I ached for him. Each of us was feeling the bitter, lonely pain and dealing with Angela's sudden death the best we knew how. I was glad to see that Keith had finally fallen asleep. I climbed back into bed, hoping to find relief. My mind continued to be filled with thoughts of Angela.

> *I thought of you as I walked the shore,*
> *Watching the sunset and saw new doors.*
> *I thought of how we must go on,*
> *And forget the dreams of us being one.*
> *There will be a time when we will depart,*
> *Our laughter and tears will fade in the dark.*
> *I hurt so bad that not even you could understand.*
> *But we must put our memories behind,*
> *Forget the good and bad times.*
> *Take a step forward,*
> *Don't look back,*
> *Because I won't be back!*
>
> *Angela, FREE BIRD*

Chapter Three

SO MUCH PAIN WITHIN

"The LORD upholds all those who fall and lifts up all who are bowed down." (Psalm 145:14)

Once Angela started high school, she spent less time with her "good" friends. Paula was the exception. Her new friends made Keith and me feel uneasy. We sensed by their attitude and appearance, and by Angela's unusual secretiveness and defense of them, that they were not good friends for her. After spending time with them, Angela would become moody. She tired easily, often sleeping for long periods of time. Angela's increasing rebellion bewildered us. What used to be occasional disruptions were now daily events. Her anger intensified, increasing the tension and turmoil we all felt when we were around her. I found empty beer cans in her bedroom. When we asked her about it, she denied any knowledge of it. Weeks later, I found a marijuana pipe in her bedroom closet. When Keith and I confronted her, she acted surprised that it was a pipe used for drugs.

"Is that what it is? I didn't know that. A friend at school gave it to me."

Angela had told us so many convincing lies. We wanted to believe her, but there were so many obvious signs that made us suspect that drugs and alcohol were very important to her. We grew cautious and wary, watching for any evidence of drug use.

One afternoon, Angela stormed into the house, angry and defensive. I confronted her, "Angela, I think you've been taking drugs."

"So, you have a right to your opinion, even if it's wrong."

"Have you taken any drugs today?"

"No!" she shouted. "And I can't believe you're asking me."

"I think you're lying to me. I'm going to take you to the doctors to be tested."

"You can't make me go with you."

Motioning for her brother Carl to come and help, I said, "Angela, you can get in the car by yourself or the two of us will take you to it."

She turned and angrily led the way to the car, climbing into the back seat with Carl next to her.

"I can't believe this. My own family is treating me like a criminal. This pisses me off. You're going to be sorry when you find out you spent your money for nothing."

I stopped the car after pulling into a parking space in front of the medical clinic. I turned to face her.

"Before we go inside I want you to know if the test results show that you're on drugs, you're going to pay for this test. If it doesn't, I'll pay for it and I'll owe you an apology. Now tell me before we go in, have you taken any drugs today?"

"No!" she screamed.

By this time, I wondered if I was doing the right thing, but I had to be sure. I stepped out of the car, and stood waiting for her to get out. She sat in the car, enraged, and yelled, "O.K. So I took drugs . . . big deal."

When we returned home she stomped into the house and up the stairs to her bedroom, slamming the door behind her. There was no reasoning with her.

Keith and I monitored her allowance. We gave her small amounts of money making her accountable for the money she spent. I wasn't sure when I handed her lunch money each day if it would be used for food or for drugs. The high school secretary started calling, telling me of her unexcused absences. I'd drive her to school in the morning, drop her off and watch her go into the building, only to discover later that she had waited until I drove off to leave with her friends. We were never sure where she disappeared to on those days.

I fondly remembered a time during Christmas, when Paula's mother, Mary, and I talked about taking the kids to a nursing home to learn that Christmas was for giving, not just receiving. Angela really liked the idea. We were given permission by the nurse in charge to visit their thirty-six elderly residents. Paula, Angela, Travis and Jason helped pick out thirty-six inexpensive gifts. The girls wrote '*Jesus Is The Reason For The Season*' on paper and tied each one onto the gifts. Like old times, Paula and Angela had fun baking cupcakes and stacking them into boxes before it was time to leave. The girls giggled in the back seat on the way. We had bought combs for the men and Angela asked, "What if they don't have any hair?"

A nurse was there to greet us, and she invited us to go freely from room to room. Angela took off down the hall with a bag full of gifts in her hand. I watched as she confidently approached each elderly person with an enthusiastic "Hi!" and a sincere smile. She handed them a gift and if they were unable to open it themselves, she gently took it from them, "Here, let me help you . . . And, look we made this for you, too." She pulled out the paper, and with her voice raised so they could clearly hear her, she read to them from the paper she and Paula had written, "Jesus Is The Reason For The Season." She spent time with each elderly person. She hugged some of them before leaving their room. "Bye," she said, "Have a happy Christmas." She left them with grateful smiles on their faces. In the hallway there was an elderly woman who sat in her wheelchair. Her thin white hair hung uncombed around her face. She was leaning over in her wheelchair. Her eyes were intently fixed on Angela. She grunted as Angela came toward her and without hesitation, Angela hurried to the woman, carefully setting a gift on her lap by her folded hands. She gently spoke to the lady before moving on.

We left, each of us feeling good about our visit. I was amazed by Angela's tenderness, and sensitivity shown toward these elderly people. This was the happiest and most free I had seen my daughter in a long time. I encouraged her that we could continue going back to the home to visit.

"It was fun," she said, "but I don't want to go back."

I tucked away the memory of that day as a reminder of my special and caring little girl who hid beneath this mask of toughness and rebellion.

Life continued to be a roller coaster. Yet, there were still those precious times as Angela's tenderness surfaced when she would reach out to neighbors, like baking cookies or picking roses to give to others; just to make them happy.

But more often, we felt overwhelmed by the magnitude of the ongoing crises. Her absences from school increased. One day she didn't come home from school. Keith and I frantically searched for her. Later that night, we found her at a girlfriend's home.

"I don't want to go home. You're always telling me what to do. Just wait," she said as she climbed into the car. "I'll take off again, and next time you won't be able to find me."

That was the beginning of many runaways. At the age of fourteen, Angela frequently didn't come home from school and often left in the middle of the night. We would awake in the morning to find her missing. Each time she became more skillful in planning her runaways, making sure we couldn't find her.

My sister, Mary, and my brother-in-law, Joe, expressed their concern and offered to let Angela stay with them to see if that might help.

Surely, we could work things out, I thought. But, things only became worse. There were nights I heard that Angela had slept behind convenience stores after taking drugs from people she met, and God only knows what else took place.

We decided to let her go to Mary and Joe's. I struggled with feelings of failure and wondered how Angela would feel if we insisted she live with Mary and Joe instead of being at home with us, but we had to do what was best for her. Mary and Joe loved Angela; they sincerely wanted to help and Angela was fond of them. She would only be an hour's drive away from our home. Maybe by staying with them for a period of time, it could be a new beginning for her; maybe it would break the vicious cycle of her running away.

We didn't tell Angela ahead of time. Mary, Joe, Keith and I walked into her bedroom one evening after she had threatened to run away again. She looked up in surprise when the four of us entered.

"Angela," Keith said, "you're going to be living with Mary and Joe for a while."

She appeared dumbfounded. She studied our faces to see if we were joking. The color drained from her face as it dawned on her that we were serious.

With a determined yet shaky voice, she answered, "I don't want to live over there. This is my home."

Keith spoke, "Angela, this is for your own good. We can't have you running away every time you don't like something that's said or done around here."

"We're going to pack your clothes, and take you home with us," Joe said.

"Tonight?"

"Yes, tonight," he answered.

Helplessly, she watched us put her belongings into bags and suitcases. Joe and Keith carried them to the car. I felt like a traitor as I watched her follow them to the car.

Angela started to climb into the back seat. Sensing how hard this was for Angela, Mary took her by the arm. "Angela, you can sit up front with me."

They squeezed into the front seat together. Keith and I stood in the driveway as their car pulled away. Angela turned her head in our direction. A confused, hurting little girl stared back at me. I rushed into the house sobbing, feeling her pain and my own. What else could we do?

Mary, Joe and their children, Lisa, Kevin, and David graciously welcomed Angela. Mary enrolled Angela in their local high school. Her attitude in their home was better than it had been in a long time. She and her cousin, David, became very close during that time. Kevin, David, and Lisa introduced Angela to their friends, who also reached out to her. We were all encouraged by her progress.

Even though Angela struggled with her classes, she made an effort to do her best and her grades improved. Unfortunately, she soon made friends with students who were known drug users. She began skipping school, and she and a boy were accused of smoking marijuana during the lunch hour. Her grades dropped to D's and F's, and a few teachers complained of her disruptiveness in class. Six weeks after she had enrolled in school, Mary and I attended a meeting that was called to decide if Angela would be allowed to continue attending their high school. The administrators decided to let her finish the semester. In the summer Angela returned home.

> *I feel so much love yet I want to get out.*
> *I have so much pain within me no doubt.*
> *I feel security but I just don't care.*
> *I want to be free . . . just let me be.*
> *Angela, FREE BIRD*

CHAPTER FOUR

CAN THIS BE REALITY?

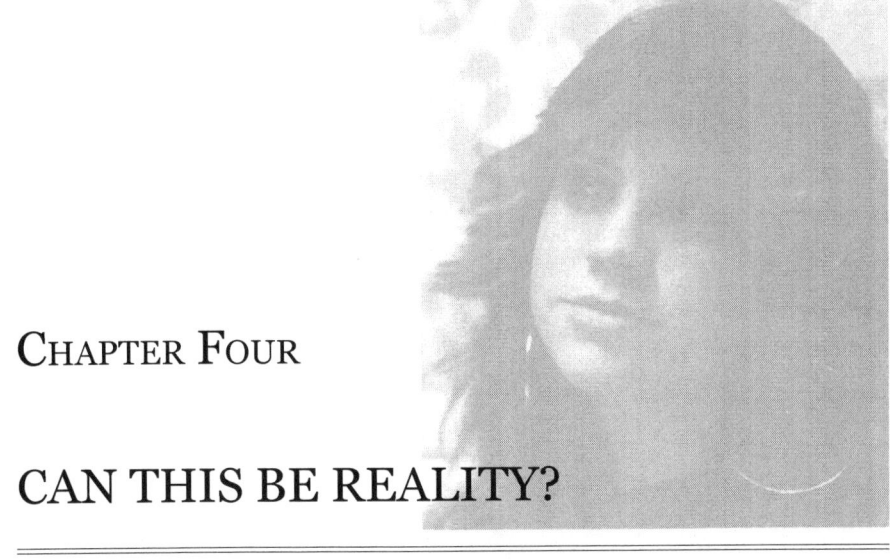

"Be still, and know that I am God . . ."
(Psalm 46:10)

Wanting to find help and not knowing where else to turn, we started attending a group called *Tough Love*. The support and concern we received from other parents who had struggled as we did gave us a glimmer of hope. We shared our frustrations about Angela, our knowledge of her drug usage, her continual runaways, her lying, and her increasing rebellion. But as we continued to attend the meetings, we realized the solutions that were working for other parents weren't working for us or for Angela. On the contrary, deeper problems were surfacing.

Angela was now telling me she saw a demon at a friend's house.

"Mom, they have a real demon in their house and it does nice things for them."

Alarmed, but cautious about her story, I listened and asked for more information.

"They told me a little girl died in that house before they moved in. They think it's the girl's spirit. When they go to bed at night, they don't lock their doors, because it does it for them.

I saw it happen!" Fascinated by what she saw she also told me, "Demons aren't bad; they're nice and friendly to people."

A few days later as I carried Angela's clothes to her bedroom, I found a paper sitting on Angela's desk that caught my attention. There was a picture of a drawn figure labeled, *'Mom'*. Next to it was a picture of a demon with horns with the caption that said *'Satan, Kill Her'*. The demon carried a long sword, blood dripping from it, directed toward the figure labeled *'Mom'*. When I asked Angela about it she said, "Yes, that's you." There was no embarrassment. She seemed happy that I had found it.

That night I sat on her bed rubbing her back. This was one of those rare times she let me do it.

She said to me, "Promise me you won't tell anyone. It's kind of scary, but sometimes I hear a voice telling me to do mean things."

Startled, I asked, "What kind of mean things?"

"Usually, it tells me to hurt people."

"When do you hear this voice?"

"When I'm angry I hear it."

A few days after our conversation, I walked in the front door, returning from a shopping trip. Broken glass was on the hallway floor, and chairs were turned on their side in the kitchen.

"What's going on?"

Carl came in the door behind me shaken and upset.

"What happened?" I asked.

"After you left, Angela went to Chuck's house. She was gone for over an hour."

Chuck was one of her new *'friends'* whom we suspected was providing drugs for Angela.

Carl continued, "She came home and started fighting with me. I told her to stop, but she wouldn't. I fought back." He told me how she had grabbed the antique rifle that sat on the fireplace and started swinging it at him. He continued, "She chased me outside and locked the doors. She got a knife from the kitchen drawer and said she'd kill me if I tried to come in!"

Just then Angela stormed into the room. "Carl, I hate you! You're the biggest liar! You've got to go running to Mommy and tell her everything."

"Stop it!" I demanded. She admitted she had chased Carl with a rifle. Yes, she knocked the chairs over, and she assured me she would do it again if she had to. I found knife marks in the wood of the kitchen cabinets.

Carl, Travis, and Jason told Keith and me about their increasing resentment toward her. If the kids were left home for any length of time, Angela would often change the channels or bring the phone into the den and talk loud enough to her friends so the boys couldn't hear the television or each other, and then dare them to do anything about it. If they stood up to her, there would be a fight. If she lost, she would sneak upstairs to their rooms and destroy one of their prized possessions.

All our lives were being affected. Often I felt like I was on the front lines of a battlefield fighting a war I couldn't win. Angela knew how to push my buttons. I wanted her to know I loved her, but more often now I reacted in anger and frustration toward her. One time when she argued with me and mocked me, I lost control and slapped her face. I instantly felt shame and remorse. Shocked, and then angry, she smiled at me with a smugness that communicated she had won.

The tension increased, and my patience wore thin. Each day there was a new crisis. Then, one evening we received this phone call:

"Mrs. Noe? This is the sheriff's department. Your daughter, Angela, has been arrested for shoplifting."

The officer told me where to meet him. Within minutes, Keith and I arrived at the department store, and an employee directed us to a back room where Angela sat in a chair off to the side. Her eyes met ours, and then quickly looked away. A sheriff stood up and walked toward us.

"Mr. and Mrs. Noe?"

We nodded. He led us to a small storage room.

"I can release your daughter to you since this is her first arrest, or we can take her in and book her. We could let her sit there for a couple of hours, and you could pick her up later tonight."

Once he assured us of her safety, Keith and I knew what we had to do. We had talked about it on the way to the store. Angela had lied and manipulated her way out of so many other situations, avoiding the consequences. Believing we were doing the right thing, we told him to take her in. We walked over and sat next to Angela. I tried to hide my surprise when I saw the handcuffs locked around her wrists. She was so young, only fifteen years old. I ached for her. I put my arms around her. This time she didn't pull away.

"So what are they going to do to me?"

"They're going to take you to jail. They'll call us when it's time to pick you up."

"How long will that be?"

"I don't know for sure."

A young woman in her twenties sat across from us. She sat limp in her chair with her head hanging down. She also was handcuffed. The sheriff motioned for us to leave.

"We have to go, Angela."

After hugging her, we reluctantly left, hoping this might help her see the wrong direction in which she was headed.

Time passed slowly that night. We kept watching the clock, waiting for the phone call from the sheriff. Finally, at midnight, he called and Keith left to pick her up. While driving home from the police station, Angela complained to Keith that she wasn't able to sleep in that dumb, noisy jail. She scolded her dad for not warning her that she would be arrested if she was caught shoplifting. Later, we heard from friends that she bragged about her jail experience to her peers the next day. Sadly, we realized this experience had no great impact on her.

Soon after, I discovered further upsetting news. One evening, after dinner, Travis came into the kitchen and said to me, "Mom, come upstairs with me. But we need to be quiet."

I followed him, wondering what the great suspense was. We stopped outside the closed bathroom door. We could hear Angela heaving inside the bathroom.

Before I could speak, Travis led me into my bedroom.

"Angela's been doing this every night for a long time. She stuffs herself, and then goes upstairs and throws up."

When I asked Angela about these nightly incidents she was embarrassed and angry that I knew, and refused to talk about it.

Another night, I found her in the bathroom with the door open and a razor blade in her hand cutting swastika symbols on her arms.

"Angela! What are you doing?" I yelled.

She looked at me defiantly. "I'm cutting my arm."

She put the razor blade down, and walked out of the bathroom. Her arm was bright red where she had cut.

"You want to know why I'm cutting my arms?" She glared at me. "Because if I didn't cut myself, I'd have to cut you! That's why!"

With that, she stormed into her bedroom, slamming the door behind her.

Did I need to fear for my life in my own home? Fighting tears, I wondered how it had gotten this severe. What would it take to reach her? There didn't seem to be any answers.

As I sat in our *Tough Love* group telling of these most recent events, there was an awkward silence. There was no usual brainstorming for ideas for us tonight. They told Keith and me what we already knew.

"You need to get psychological help for her."

Just the week before, I had read in the newspaper of a psychological hospital that also tested women for hormonal imbalances. We wanted to find help for the many surfacing problems, but this was one area we hadn't investigated yet. Keith and I agreed that I should set up an appointment for her to be tested for P.M.S. and also talk with the psychologist to get his professional opinion.

I called the hospital the next morning. I shared some of our struggles and concerns on the phone and made an appointment for Angela to be tested and to see the psychologist. I explained to Angela why we were going, while expressing my hopes it might help her. She was willing.

When Angela and I arrived, we announced ourselves to the receptionist and waited to be called. We both felt uneasy sitting on the outdated couch in that small, bleak room.

"So, this is where the crazies are, huh?" She surveyed the room. Her foot started moving nervously. "I don't like it here."

Neither did I. The doctor, a tall man in his mid-fifties, appeared and greeted us. After talking with us for a few minutes, he asked if he could speak with Angela alone.

It seemed like an eternity before he returned. He led me to the conference room where Angela sat across from his desk.

"Please sit down," he said.

I sat in the leather chair next to Angela.

"I believe there are some serious problems Angela needs help with. I'm sure she could benefit by staying in our adolescent program."

"You mean stay here?" I said.

Surprised, I looked at Angela whose eyes were getting bigger. She frantically glanced from me to him.

"Angela wouldn't miss any school," he said. We have our own school, and she would see a counselor daily and be involved in group therapy. We have a variety of activities for the teenagers including swimming, sports, and field trips."

He spoke to me, "You will also have family therapy."

Then he asked Angela, "Would you like me to have someone show you our facilities while I talk with your mom?"

"I guess I can take a look at it," she said.

A friendly, older woman came through the door and took Angela with her.

The doctor proceeded to tell me what I already knew, "Your daughter's in trouble. Her self-destructive choices are taking her on a fast downward spiral."

I knew he was right. It didn't take much for him to convince me she needed more help than we could give her. But, should we admit her into this mental hospital?

Angela surprised me when she returned with a big grin. "I'm willing to try it."

I called Keith and asked him to meet us at the hospital immediately. After the doctor communicated his concern for Angela, and the benefits of the program to Keith and me, he left us alone to decide. Keith and I, painfully aware of the intensity and frequency of the crises, felt torn. We decided if Angela agreed to stay, we'd sign the admittance papers. Hoping this was the right choice, we said goodbye to her. Angela's only worry seemed to be that we would forget to bring all of her belongings back to the hospital.

Tears fell as I drove home in a daze, wondering if this was the best thing for Angela. But what else could we do? Too many nights she had run away and we didn't know where she was or with whom she was staying for days at a time. At least by admitting her into this hospital we'd know her whereabouts. Also, she'd receive daily counseling here, and we'd have family therapy which would benefit all of us. It couldn't hurt, or could it? It was hard to believe I had taken her to the hospital this morning for a simple test and consultation and a few hours later I was driving home without her.

When I got home, I explained to the boys that we had left Angela at the hospital. They understood she needed help.

After talking to the boys, I immediately took a suitcase into Angela's bedroom and packed the items she had asked for: her bedspread, her pillow, and her stuffed animals. I also picked up her favorite teddy bear that she asked us to bring. There was such a sensitive, and tender, little girl inside that hard shell. Why wouldn't she let us in? It hurt that we had not been getting along. It hurt that my love for her could not make things better like it used to when she was younger. I wondered what she was feeling at this moment, and how she would feel when she climbed into bed tonight being confined in a strange place. I quickly finished packing. Maybe she would feel less afraid with her possessions next to her.

That night, Keith and I fell into bed physically and emotionally drained. Neither of us slept well. Life was becoming too complicated.

> *This is a world that confuses me.*
> *I don't understand . . . Can this be reality?*
> *Or is this just me?*
> *I'm standing in the middle of nowhere,*
> *Wondering if I was meant to be here.*

Farewell, My Free Bird

I just laugh my way through life.
There is many here among us who feel life is a joke.
And it's not a phase,
It's something I feel every day.
I want to pull myself out of this world with my mind.
I want to exist in a different world.
Somewhere that doesn't have time.
                          Angela, FREE BIRD

Chapter Five

WHY CAN'T THE WORLD LET ME BE?

"Trust in the LORD with all your heart and lean not on your own understanding; in all your ways acknowledge Him, and He will make your paths straight." (Proverbs 3:5-6)

The next day, our reservations about Angela being in the hospital were relieved when we saw her. She ran up to us and gave us a hug. She introduced us to her roommate, and then together they left for the gym to play basketball. We found the room for our first meeting with the psychologist. Once it began, parents talked of similar heartaches with their teenagers. It helped us to know we weren't alone. We left the hospital feeling confident that we had made the right decision.

The next night, we arrived at the hospital looking forward to spending time with Angela. A young man led us down a long hall into a well-lit, spacious cafeteria. We followed him into an outside courtyard. Right in front of us, positioned in the center of the courtyard, was a large building. A row of narrow buildings was on the right; to the left, a swimming pool enclosed by a high chain link fence. We stepped up a small ramp, and stood at the door of this large building and waited. He fumbled with his keys and unlocked the heavily secured door. We crowded into a cramped room and faced another locked door with a thick glass pane. I felt uneasy and my confidence about her being here dwindled while we stood waiting for this second door to be opened. It didn't seem right for her to be locked up. An older lady, tall and thin, pressed the buzzer from under her desk to let us in. It was strangely quiet.

The young man introduced us.

Her quick smile was very business-like.

"Angela's been waiting for you. The other teenagers just left for an Alcoholics Anonymous meeting. If these are Angela's belongings I need to inspect them."

I handed her the bag of extra clothes and personal items for Angela.

I turned and saw Angela coming toward us.

We hugged. I could tell by her frown that she wasn't feeling as cheerful tonight.

"Can I show my mom and dad my room?"

"Sure."

She led us down a long hall to the second door on the left, to a tiny room with two twin beds, one on either side of the window. Her stuffed animals were carefully placed on her bedspread. Her pictures were hung on the wall.

"Your room looks nice," I said.

"They won't let me shut my door because you told them I cut myself with the razor. That's why they put me in a room close to the front desk. I still need my radio. Did you bring everything I asked you to?"

"I brought everything you asked for, but it has to be checked at the desk first."

"They'd better give it to me. They already said I could have it." She stepped outside her room into the hallway. "We can't stay in here. We have to go somewhere else to visit."

The woman led us to a side door and again we found ourselves outside going up an extended ramp. We entered what looked like a recreation room with a pool table. Small tables and chairs were dispersed throughout the room.

"Will you buy me a soda, Dad?"

"Sure." Keith dug for change in his pocket. We sat down. The lady remained outside, watching and apparently listening to our conversation.

Angela immediately started telling us of her displeasure, "I don't like it here."

"What don't you like about it?" Keith asked.

"They have a dumb school. The counseling is good. I'm getting to know some of the kids. I like my roommate."

"That's good. Why is she here?"

"For taking drugs and running away. Her parents are messed up, but she's cool. Most of these kids are in here for drugs. One guy is totally wasted. He took an overdose. He may never come out of it. My friend said she was supposed to be here for only two weeks, and she's been here for two months. I don't want to stay here anymore!"

"Angela," I answered, "you said you would be willing to try it."

"This is a place for crazies, and I'm not crazy!"

"No one said you were crazy." Keith tried to reassure her. "Don't you think there are teenagers here who just need help working through problems?"

"I don't belong here!"

"Angela, you need help. That's why you're here."

"I don't have any problems, you do. I agreed to come in here. If you don't get me out, I'll find a way out!" She glared at us; her face tense, her eyes filled with anger and frustration. "You fucking bitches, I hate you!" She abruptly stood up, knocking the table over on its side. Her drink flew across the table and landed on my leg. Keith and I stared at Angela in disbelief. In an instant, the woman was in the room taking control.

"Angela, it's time to go back now."

I was stunned. My pant leg was dripping wet and cold. We followed them back. Angela defiantly walked ahead of us, and when we entered the building she headed for her room.

"You'll have to leave," the woman said.

She motioned to the young man to let us out. Perplexed, we waited as he unlocked the door. I glanced at Angela's treasured possessions still in a bag on the desk. We heard a loud crash coming from the direction of her room. As the lady hurried down the hall to check on Angela, we were swiftly escorted out through the double locked doors.

We left the hospital discouraged, bewildered and hurting. It was evident that Angela desperately needed help, but was this hospital the answer?

"Keith, what are we going to do?"

"What else *can* we do?"

"I don't know," I answered. "I understand her feelings about being here, and her anger about being locked up," I said, "but if we let her come home she'll run again. At least we know she's safe here at the hospital and she's getting the help she needs."

"If only she would just stop fighting everything and everyone!" Keith was angry. We both felt helpless.

We called the hospital when we arrived home; they assured us Angela was alright.

One night during that week, we decided we needed to spend an evening at home with the boys. Angela needed special attention, especially now, but we also needed to be sure we didn't neglect our sons. We told Angela we wouldn't be coming that night.

It was eleven p.m. Keith and I had just fallen asleep when we were awakened by the sound of the phone ringing. I groped in the dark to find the receiver.

"Hello."

"Mrs. Noe? This is the hospital. Angela has run away."

"Run away? How could she have run away?" I thought of the double locked doors and the tall fences surrounding the area.

"She and her roommate broke the window, and before we could get to them they had climbed over the fence and run off into the night. We are in the process of making out a police report. We'll call you if we hear anything."

Keith and I were in disbelief. We, mistakenly, had assumed she was safe there. I felt sick inside. What is she going to do? It's late. I tossed and turned, praying for her protection. At 2 a.m., the phone rang again.

"Hello. Mom?"

"Angela? Where are you?"

"Do you know that I ran away?"

"Yes. Where are you?"

"If I tell you, will you pick me up and take me back to the hospital?"

I was stunned at her request. "You want to go back?"

"Yes."

"Alright, tell me where you are."

I picked her up a couple of blocks from our house. She stood alone near the phone booth in a dark, deserted shopping center. She wouldn't tell me where she had been or where her friend was. She just wanted to go back to the hospital without any explanation. I was so confused, yet encouraged that she wanted to go back. Maybe now she would stop resisting, and this could be a new beginning for all of us.

To our dismay, nothing changed. Her pattern of resistance continued stronger than ever. In school, she answered the teacher's questions by writing profanities in bold letters across her papers. She refused to cooperate with their rules. Even her peers in the hospital attempted to reason with her, but she wouldn't listen to them. The staff related to us that they had never had anyone as *'smooth'* as she. They told us that the normal procedures that usually work for the other teenagers weren't working for her. It alarmed me when they spoke of her as their greatest challenge. It didn't take the therapist long before he learned he had to check with other staff members first before he believed what Angela told him. He also had been tricked by her deceptions. She gave the doctor a run for his money, cursing him like an experienced sailor every time she spoke with him, determined not to cooperate with the rules he set.

The longer she remained in the hospital the more evident it became to all of us she needed help, and the angrier she became at us for keeping her there.

She ran again by climbing over the fence, but this time by herself. For a few days we didn't know where she was. Diane, a good friend of Angela's, called to tell us she had heard from her.

"I don't know what's really true, but Angela called me just a few minutes ago. She said you and Keith don't care about her, and the reason she's living out on the street is because you won't let her come home."

"Diane, we love her and we care about her. We're trying to get help for her, so she can come home."

"Well, that's what I thought. I'm afraid for her. She told me that last night she spent the night with a man she had just met. Right now, she's at the Winchell's Donut Shop deciding where to go next. I thought you should know."

Keith and I hopped in the car and sped to the place she had directed us to. We slowly drove from the busy street into the parking lot. I saw her through the window, sitting at a table with her black hat on, drinking a cup of coffee. She looked so lost and so young. Angela saw us get out of the car. Surprised, she bolted up from her chair and rushed to the door. We hurried to stop her before she could leave.

"So, how did you find me? Why don't you just leave me alone and let me do what I want?"

"Angela, we're not going to leave you alone to destroy yourself."

"You don't care about me. You just care about yourselves."

We led her to the car.

I jumped in the back seat first, quickly setting the child safety lock, in case she fought us or tried to jump out. Keith waited until Angela climbed in next to me. I put my arm around my fifteen year old daughter. She didn't respond, but she didn't resist. On the way to the hospital, we listened to her anger and to an occasional string of profanities. Telling her we loved her didn't seem to make any difference. She was wound up like a top. We checked her into the hospital and left feeling totally wiped out.

Days and months wore on. I struggled with depression as the circumstances worsened. Experiencing one crisis after another had drained me physically and emotionally. It was taking its toll on all of us.

One morning, I sat at the kitchen table, devastated, seeing no hope for Angela's future. She was out of control, and we were all suffering. I sat with a Bible in front of me. I opened it and started reading Psalm 107. When I came to verse 10, the words seemed to come alive, and remained like that until I finished reading verse 22. I didn't hear an audible voice, but in my mind, I heard words spoken as clearly and real as if they had been audible, *"I'm giving you these promises for Angela."* At the same time the words were spoken, an overwhelming peace filled me. I read the Scriptures again, but this time with new meaning, knowing these words were given to me from God for Angela.

> *"Some sat in darkness and the deepest gloom, prisoners suffering in iron chains, for they had rebelled against the words of God and despised the counsel of the most High. So He subjected them to bitter labor; they stumbled, and there was no one to help. Then, they cried out to the Lord in their trouble and He saved them from their distress. He brought them out of darkness and the deepest gloom and broke away their chains. Let them give thanks to the Lord for His unfailing love and His wonderful deeds for men, for He breaks down gates of bronze and cuts through bars of iron. Some became fools through their rebellious ways and suffered affliction because of their iniquities. They loathed all food and drew near the gates of death. Then, they cried to the Lord in their trouble, and He saved them from distress. He sent forth His word and healed them. He rescued them from the grave. Let them give thanks to the Lord for His unfailing love and His wonderful deeds for men. Let them sacrifice thank offerings and tell of His works with songs of joy."*

I continued reading in the Psalms. When reading Psalm 103, verses 3-5, the words came alive once again.

> *"He forgives all my sins and heals all my diseases; He redeems my life from the pit and crowns me with love and compassion. He satisfies my desires with good things, so that my youth is renewed like the eagles."*

I dated these Scriptures, April 4, 1984, knowing they were promises for my daughter from God. The circumstances didn't change, but now I had hope and something from the Lord I could hold onto. I knew He was going to work in her life.

Angela's lack of obedience at the hospital and her continual runaways had forced the staff to put her in their Intensive Care Unit. This unit was even more securely locked than the building the teenagers stayed in. She continually refused to cooperate, even though she knew she could return to be with her peers if she would only be willing to try.

On April 8th, while in the Intensive Care Unit, Angela turned sixteen. We had special permission from the doctor to bring the family to the hospital and celebrate her birthday. Keith and I and her grandparents, great grandmother, and brothers entered the locked facility to make our best effort to celebrate Angela's sixteenth birthday.

Great Grandma Hunt, elderly and barely able to walk, determinedly walked the long distance from the parking lot and down the long halls. We slowed our pace to match hers. She approached the locked doors, stopped, and shook her head.

"It's such a pity," she said.

Angela and her great grandma had a very special relationship. Grandma's heart was breaking for her much-loved granddaughter. Bewildered, she asked the question we all asked, "Why?"

I carried a large, decorated cake with Angela's name on it. Our presents were carefully chosen. Money was eliminated as an option, as was any other gift that might be used to buy drugs. Light jesting, singing "Happy Birthday" to her while other patients joined in, were our attempts to make it fun for her. She seemed appreciative, and participated in the pretense that this was a time to celebrate. We weren't allowed to stay long. We left her with smiles, hugs, and assurances of our love. Angela followed us as far as she could to the exit. Great Grandma, with tears glistening in her eyes, paused and took Angela's hand in hers.

"Angela, I want you to know I love you no matter what. You be a good girl for me. Promise me you'll try your best."

"I will, Grandma." They were both teary when they embraced and said goodbye.

We drove out of the hospital parking lot, each struggling with our own despair and sadness.

The next day, Angela and another patient accosted two female employees who were delivering food trays to the ICU. They knocked the trays down and escaped through the partially opened doors, once again disappearing into the streets. We didn't know Angela's whereabouts for days.

A few nights later, I picked up the phone and heard her voice, soft and quiet. "Mom?"

"Angela? Are you O.K.?"

"Yes. That's why I called, to tell you I'm alright." I heard a man's voice in the background.

"Who is that with you?"

"It's someone I met today. He's letting me stay here for the night."

I detected fear in her voice.

Farewell, My Free Bird

"Where are you?"

"I can't tell you. I just wanted you to know I'm alright."

It would do no good to push her for details. I knew she would hang up on me.

"Are you safe, Angela?"

"Yes." She didn't sound convincing.

"Why don't you let me pick you up?"

"No. I've got to go now."

"I love you, Angela."

"I love you too, Mom. Bye."

I hung up the phone feeling helpless, sensing her pain, but not understanding the dynamics of her rebellion. Why? Why is this happening? *God, keep her safe. You're the only one who can help her!* I was gently reminded of the Scriptures He had given me, and how at this very moment God knew where she was and He had His eye upon her. He could be there for her when I couldn't. Somehow with that knowledge I gained enough peace to close my eyes and get a few hours of sleep.

She returned to the hospital on her own the next day. Her counselor told me, "It's a miracle your daughter's alive."

"I know." I said, painfully aware of the truth of his words.

In June, plans were made for a family wedding. We were given a one day pass for Angela to be there. She was so happy to be able to go. At the reception, music and dancing were planned until late in the evening. Grandma Hunt was there and anytime she lost sight of Angela she became anxious. Once she stopped me as I walked by her, "Carol, I haven't seen Angela." Before I could tell her she was in the hallway, she gripped my arm and said, "Carol, she's gone, isn't she? Tell me the truth."

"Grandma, she's here. I just saw her."

"Are you sure you're not just telling me that?"

"I promise you; I'm telling you the truth. Wait here and I'll have her come and see you."

Angela sat at a small table near the entrance of the reception hall.

"Angela, come in here. Grandma hasn't seen you for a while and she's worried about you."

Angela would do anything for Grandma. She immediately went over to her, hugging her, and assuring her she wouldn't run off.

Grandma Hunt, exhausted from the long day, went home early. Angela disappeared. Several of us went looking for her and eventually found her in an intimate embrace with a boy she had just met. She reeked of alcohol. Exasperated, we hurried to get her back to the hospital, barely arriving before her eight-hour pass expired.

The next morning, the doctor, his patience worn thin, called to inform us he was releasing Angela because of her alcohol consumption the night before. He would not bend. He instructed us to pick her up before the day was over. I hung up feeling mixed emotions. On a day-to-day basis the family had gotten used to living without the constant turmoil. Angela had not improved. If anything, the circumstances had worsened.

Needless to say, Angela was thrilled. She said goodbye triumphantly to her friends while we loaded the trunk of the car with her belongings.

I wanted to be happy she was returning home, but instead, I was fearful and apprehensive for what was ahead.

> *I can see in this world everyone is in their own brain,*
> *I can feel the way they can't hang.*
> *Everyone's so into power and it's driving me insane.*
> *Kick back and enjoy life before it's too late.*
> *Where is all the love and peace?*

Farewell, My Free Bird

It's all turned to hate.
I want to be free from your little world,
And your stupid games.
I want to fly to the moon,
And crawl inside purple pyramids,
And smoke camel non-filters and go insane.
I want to be free on LSD.
Why can't this world let me be?
Let me be free!
                             Angela, FREE BIRD

Chapter Six

I TRY TO FIT IN BUT I CAN'T

> *"Why are you downcast, O my soul? Why so disturbed within me? Put your hope in God, for I will yet praise Him, my Savior and my God." (Psalm 42:5)*

Angela eagerly unpacked, happy to be home and in her own room again, arranging her cherished possessions, putting each item in its place to her satisfaction. She told us how much she appreciated being home. There were still problems to work through, but the intense anxiety I had felt about Angela coming home softened. I began to feel a glimmer of hope.

But even before the week ended, it proved to be a false hope. Outbursts of anger, taking off impulsively and drug use plagued us once again. There was no respect for the family. The battle raged on, picking up where it had left off before we admitted her to the hospital, this time with a heightened intensity.

Angela came home one afternoon pleased with a new tattoo. Imprinted on her left shoulder was a tattoo that said, 'Free Bird.'

She told me, "Mom, ever since I was a little girl, I've wanted to be a free bird and do my own thing."

Days later, she called me into her bedroom.

"Listen! This is my favorite song. It's called *'Free Bird!'*" She turned the volume up. I watched her listen with delight to the words that were being sung. She so desperately desired to be free, yet her individual search for freedom was leading her to the wrong places and to the wrong people. Her search for freedom was slowly destroying her.

We continued after-care counseling at the hospital but had to cancel several appointments since Angela often disappeared from home for days to be with her *'friends'* or strangers she had met out on the streets. One night we picked her up at the sheriff's department. We had reported her missing. Two days later the sheriff's department called to tell us they had found Angela at her friend Tina's home, sleeping in Tina's bedroom closet, huddled on top of a pile of clothes, drunk. The girls had marijuana on them. At midnight we arrived at the station and identified ourselves as Angela's parents.

The sheriff escorted Angela to the front desk, and directed her to a wooden bench. "Sit down right here while I finish making out this report."

She looked disheveled and weary. She had always been meticulous about her hair, keeping it clean and combed to perfection. Tonight, her clothes were wrinkled, and her hair unkempt.

Keith, also exhausted, walked toward her in despair. "Angela, for God's sake, when is this going to stop? You can't keep running off like this."

Angela instantly shot back at him, "You're just a dumb cop! You don't know anything. Don't tell me what to do."

Furious, Keith grabbed her by the hair, "Don't you talk to me like that."

"I'll talk to you any way I want."

The sheriff interrupted, "Young lady, that'll be enough! You are still under our custody until I release you."

Angela started to react in anger to the sheriff, but instead, leaned back on the bench and quieted down.

The following day, Keith and I drove her to the therapist's office. We sat outside in the hallway while Angela kept her appointment with him. Almost an hour later, the therapist called us into his office to inform us that he had to report Keith to the Social Services. Stunned, we sat listening to him tell us of his obligation to report any physical violence. Keith's reaction of grabbing Angela's hair the night before was considered abuse, he said.

I looked at him, amazed. "You must be kidding!"

"No, I'm not. This is something the law requires me to do."

This was the same counselor who knew what we had been through. How could he do this? Overwhelming anger rose up within me at the injustice of it. I looked over at Keith, waiting for his reaction, but he said nothing in reply to this therapist whom I felt had betrayed us. I was trembling when we walked from his office to the car.

Angela was quick to say, "I didn't know he'd make out a report. I just told him what happened last night."

It was several days before the Social Service agent showed up at our home. Our oldest son, Carl, heard about what had happened and insisted on being in the room with us. Keith and I related the escalating problems with Angela we had dealt with for the last few years and the help we tried to get for her.

He glanced at Carl, who was ready to speak in our defense if necessary, took a few notes, thanked us for our time and left. We heard nothing more from him.

I called Angela's therapist and told him she wouldn't be back. "We've put out all this effort, time, and money, and Angela has fought every chance she's had to get help. We've gone through all this pain only to have an unjustified child abuse report made out on us. I'm sorry, but we refuse to be that vulnerable again. If Angela wants help, there are several support groups she can go to that are free. It's up to her now."

She didn't return to him for counseling, and I decided I wouldn't rescue her anymore. I wouldn't chase after her when she ran. She would have to suffer the consequences of her own actions.

Oftentimes, when she ran, she'd call in the early morning hours asking to be picked up whenever she decided she was ready to come home. This time, she phoned from Riverside, pleading with me to come and get her. Determined to be strong, I refused.

"Why should I pick you up? You seem to have no trouble getting to your destination. Why can't you find your way home just as easily?"

She knew the words to say to make me feel guilty and tug at my mother's heart.

"What am I going to do if you don't pick me up? It's two in the morning, and I'm out here alone."

"You should have thought of that before you left."

"I'm scared, Mom. Please come and get me."

I was weakening. But I couldn't let her know. This time, her manipulation wouldn't work on me no matter how hard it was for me to say no to her.

"Oh Mom! There's a man in a green car. This is the second time he's driven around the block. He's driving slowly and he's watching me."

I heard the fear in her voice.

Farewell, My Free Bird

"Where are you? Is there a store or a gas station open near you?"

"No. Everything's closed and I'm the only one out here. Here he comes again! What am I going to do?"

I wasn't sure if she was telling the truth, but how could I take that chance? If she was in danger, I needed to act quickly.

"Angela, do you know where you are? Can you give me an address?"

She read the address off the gas station sign next to the phone booth.

"Give me your phone number. Listen to me carefully. I won't be able to get to you fast enough. I'm going to call the Riverside Police Station, tell them where you are, and have the police pick you up. Don't leave the phone booth. Pretend you're talking until they arrive."

I really became alarmed when she didn't resist my idea.

She replied, "Mom, tell them to hurry."

I phoned the Riverside Police Department, giving them the information, urging them to get to her quickly. Keith was sleeping soundly and needed to get up for his job as a police officer in just a few hours. Someone needed to be here for the boys. I woke Keith just enough to let him know that I was leaving to get Angela.

I drove the car to Riverside in the wee hours of the morning, praying for her safety. By the time I arrived, the police had Angela in their custody. The policeman never saw a man in a green car, and I never knew if she lied to me. All that mattered at that moment was that she was with me and that she was safe. We left the police station and within minutes she was sound asleep. I glanced over at my sixteen-year-old daughter curled up in a ball, sleeping like a baby. She looked so innocent and helpless. My heart melted. The road became blurry as the tears fell. I wanted to hold her and rock her and make everything alright. I saw her living in an inner prison. I had so many questions that were unanswered. What was driving her? Wasn't there an answer somewhere for this extreme, bizarre behavior I witnessed in her life? I prayed as I drove back home . . . *God, give us wisdom and the grace we all need to get through this. Protect her from herself and her wrong choices and addictions that are destroying her.*

It was during this time that Carl suffered from the after effects of severe mononucleosis. He missed the last two months of his senior year in high school, which resulted in him missing his graduation ceremony. Still recovering and physically weak, he attended an adult class in the summer to complete his graduation requirements. He received his diploma in the mail. Hoping to give him some special memory of his graduation, I planned a big celebration for him at the house.

The date was set and invitations were mailed. Carl's friend, Tony, came the night before the party to spend the night at our home. After dinner, Angela asked Tony to take a walk with her. They headed for the park. While sitting on a park bench talking, a couple of male strangers approached them, and held out a bag of pills. They invited Tony and Angela to take some. Tony knew it was time to go and motioned for Angela to leave with him. Surprised, he watched Angela take the pills. Again, he tried to get her to leave.

"Go ahead without me. I'll be home later," she told him.

Not knowing what else to do, Tony came back to the house and told Carl. Carl didn't want to worry us so he decided to wait, hoping she'd be home soon. She never came home. That evening we made out a police report and spent another sleepless night waiting and wondering. Early the next morning, right after Keith left for work, I heard a knock on the front door.

I opened it to see a tall, uniformed police officer standing in front of me.

"Are you Angela Noe's mother?"

As the officer asked this question, a commotion on the street in front of our house drew my attention away from him. Standing next to a parked police car was another officer with Angela in handcuffs next to him. She was screaming at the policeman to take off the handcuffs.

"Yes, Angela's my daughter." I said, not taking my eyes off her. "Where did you find her?"

"May I come in and speak with you for a moment?"

I opened the door and led him into our living room. By this time, Carl had awakened and followed me into the room. The policeman glanced at Carl, then at me, wondering if he should continue.

"It's all right." I assured him. So much had happened already. There were no more secrets.

"We found your daughter at a local restaurant. She was going from table to table soliciting herself to the male customers."

My heart sank. I felt the tension in my body. My sixteen-year-old daughter prostituting herself? I guess I knew in my heart that Angela was prostituting herself. How could she have made it out on the streets like she did? I wanted to believe it wasn't true, but this policeman made me face reality.

"She's been drinking and we suspect she's on drugs. We had a witness who was willing to make out a report, but then he changed his mind, not wanting to get involved. We can't book her on anything unless she's taken drugs. There were two male suspects with her. When we drove up, they took off running and left her at the restaurant."

I glanced out the living room window and gazed at Angela. After the many months of her being in the hospital and going through all the intensive counseling, she was more out of control than ever. The stress was taking its toll on all of us. I looked at Carl. He was concerned for me, and I could see how embarrassed he was. His friend, Tony, had spent the night and was waiting in the next room for Carl to return with an explanation. Today was supposed to be Carl's big graduation party with family and friends, and a time for memories.

Words were hard to come by. I was angry at Angela and deeply hurt. At that moment, I was beyond aching for what she must have felt. Slowly, the words came.

"My daughter is a chronic runaway. She's incorrigible. I can't handle her. She probably is on drugs. If you release her to me, she'll be back on the streets again in a few days. I want you to take her in and book her."

He nodded. "We could take her in and have her tested, but we probably won't be able to keep her for more than a few hours."

Carl and I stood at the front door watching as the officer returned to the police car and told the other officer, "We're going to book her."

Angela started resisting. "No way! You're not taking me in. Get your dirty hands off of me," she yelled. It took both of them to force her into the car.

I watched them drive up the street with my daughter. Carl put his hand on my shoulder.

"Mom, you didn't raise her like that. Angela hasn't allowed you to teach her anything. She's let her friends raise her."

I couldn't speak. In a few hours the house would be filled with people. I thought of canceling the party, but it was too late. Besides, Carl deserved to have this celebration. I hoped somehow it could still be special for him. I decided against calling Keith at work. He would find out soon enough.

The party was difficult for me. I had to visit with family and friends and pretend that everything was fine. Several people asked about Angela. I took a deep breath, forced a smile and lied, "She's spending the weekend with a friend." If they asked too many questions about her, I excused myself to take care of the food.

Carl called me to the phone in the middle of one of those awkward conversations. A detective wanted to know when I would be coming to pick up Angela.

"I've talked to the sheriff and told him she's incorrigible," I told the detective on the phone. "It's not safe for her to be released. She'll run away again and endanger her own life."

He was impatient with me. "Mrs. Noe, this is not a babysitting service."

"I know that." I repeated what I had said before and gave him more details of what had happened before this arrest. He wasn't convinced.

"You need to come and get her right away."

"I'm sorry, but I refuse to pick her up," I answered.

He stopped for a few seconds. "If we keep her longer, you'll be charged for it."

"I understand."

"Just a moment," he said. I could hear his muffled voice on the other end.

"Mrs. Noe, I was just told that your daughter took the jacket she was wearing and tried to hang herself. We caught her before she could harm herself. We're going to keep a close eye on her. Someone will be calling you back tomorrow morning." I was shaking when I put the phone receiver down. *God, give me strength to get through the rest of this day. Put angel guards around Angela. Protect her from herself!*

When they called us the next day, we were told that because the test results showed that Angela had taken drugs, and because Angela had attempted to take her own life, she would be given a court date to appear before the judge. A few days later Keith and I were sitting on the bench outside the courtroom when the public defender approached us. He was very friendly until he realized we didn't intend to rescue Angela from the justice system. Then, his irritating personality surfaced.

"Well!" he said with disgust. "I can't believe you won't stand behind your daughter. You want to condemn her even before she's found guilty." He stared at us through his coke-bottle glasses wondering if his forceful drama had been successful. He knew our vulnerability. "If you really cared about your daughter, you would help her."

How dare this stranger insinuate we didn't care about our daughter! We repeated to him we did not want to rescue Angela.

He walked off, muttering, "I don't believe it!"

The judge, a gray-haired older man with a strong but gentle face, sat behind the bench. He listened to the evidence. Then, he asked if we wanted Angela released to us until the next trial date.

Keith stood up in the courtroom. "Your honor, I cannot guarantee that my daughter would not flee the jurisdiction of the court. I request that she be detained."

Angela appeared stunned, not expecting to hear her father insist she stay in juvenile hall. She sat next to the public defender. The color drained from her face. I felt my heart breaking as I watched her nervously wait for the judge's decision. She didn't belong here. I could feel myself weakening, but I knew we couldn't risk her running again.

The judge studied the records sitting in front of him. "I see what you mean. We have several runaway reports here. The juvenile, Angela Noe, will be held in custody until the next hearing."

She turned and looked in our direction. At that moment, I wanted to ease her pain. I wanted to be nurturing and loving. I wanted to be everything a mother was supposed to be. But, I had to sit there and do nothing, for her sake. We couldn't protect her from the consequences anymore. *Lord, Help us be strong,* I prayed. The bailiff led Angela out the side door.

I looked at Keith. "This is one of the hardest things we've ever done."

"I know, but we did the right thing," Keith said.

> I *wish I was here but my mind is gone.*
> *I try to fit in but I can't within.*
> *There is a puzzle among my head.*
> *My life is blurry and my mind is dead.*
> *I see things no one can understand.*
> *I think of things that are beyond.*
> *I and only I can comprehend.*
> *My mind is a puzzle and there's a missing piece.*
> *Angela, FREE BIRD*

Chapter Seven

I JUST WISH I WAS FREE

"Out of the goodness of Your love, deliver me. For I am poor and needy, and my heart is wounded within me." (Psalm 109:21-22)

While Keith and I drove home, I worried aloud about Angela serving time in juvenile hall.

"Do you think she'll be safe there?" I asked.

"She'll be safer there than she was out on the streets."

"And she won't have access to drugs," I reassured myself.

I sighed and leaned my head on the back of the seat. I felt empty and somewhat relieved because for a short period of time at least, I would know where Angela was.

Three days later, on Sunday afternoon, Keith and I positioned ourselves at the end of a long line that wrapped itself around the juvenile hall building. We stood with other parents who were there to visit their children. Teenagers were scattered on the grassy lawn, caring for their younger siblings while their parents went inside to visit their incarcerated brother or sister.

I missed Angela. I was eager to see her. I felt a deep sadness for her, but I also felt extremely frustrated not knowing how to reach her. I didn't know what to expect today. I assumed she'd be angry.

The guard at the door directed us to a table. We showed our identification to the lady behind the table; she checked our names off the list.

"We need to inspect your purse," she said.

I opened it, and showed her the contents.

She handed me a card with Angela's building number on it and directed us to the next table.

I carried a bag with me that contained items for Angela: shampoo, conditioner, and a magazine for her to read. The lady in front of us was unhappy with the guard because he wouldn't let her take a red toothbrush to her son.

The guard explained, "Certain colors mean certain things for gang members. Red is one of those colors. All it takes to start a fight is if someone wears or uses something in the wrong color." He set the toothbrush on the shelf behind him. "You can pick it up on the way out."

It was our turn. We stepped up. He searched the bag I handed him. He gave it back to me and pointed us in the direction of a short, heavy set male guard who stood by the locked door. This guard checked our card and started to unlock the door for us.

"Just a minute, sir," he said sternly. Keith stopped. "You're going to have to tuck in that red bandanna that's hanging out of your back pocket." The guard waited until Keith stuffed it in his pocket. Only then did he let us out.

"I've been using red bandannas long before these gang members or the guards were even born," Keith grumbled.

We stood outside looking at an immense complex with rows of buildings lined up in front of us. It took several minutes of searching before we found our way to the right one. A female guard sat behind a small table outside on the grass. She took our card and sent a young teenaged girl to get Angela. We were told to sit on the chairs that lined the sidewalk, positioning us in full view of this guard.

Angela came through the door. She looked pale and innocent and so young without her makeup. I saw her searching for us. When her eyes met ours, her face lit up into a warm smile. She hurried toward us. We embraced.

"Hi, Mom and Dad. I was praying you'd come to see me."

We sat down again with her between us.

"I guess you must be really upset with me. When I was in the courtroom and Dad told the judge that he didn't want me to come home, I thought maybe you wouldn't come today. I've had time to do a lot of thinking. I know what I did was stupid." She continued, "I went to a church service today. I didn't want to go, but it was either sitting in my room or going to church, so I went. The preacher was an ex-con. He had a hard time trying to stay straight until he accepted Jesus as his Savior and Lord. It was the turning point in his life." She asked me, "Mom, do you remember when I accepted Jesus?"

"I sure do." It was a tender memory I cherished. She was eight years old when she knelt down beside her bed and asked Jesus to forgive her of her sins and sincerely invited Him to come into her life.

She continued, "I haven't let Him be in charge. I've always wanted to do my own thing and have things my way. This morning I recommitted my life to God."

She started to cry. I hugged her and reached for tissues so we could both wipe our tears. She rested her head on my shoulder. I stroked her hair while she continued to speak of her desire for her life to be different.

It was difficult to leave her there and go home that day. Keith and I felt encouraged. We didn't doubt her sincerity, but we wondered if her resolve would last once she was released.

It wouldn't be easy for her, but we knew she could make it if she was determined and would allow God to be in control of her life.

The following week, Angela appeared before the judge again. This time, he ordered two weeks of home probation. Angela sat next to the public defender while the judge read the rules to her.

"Angela Noe, you will be required by court order to be under complete parental custody twenty-four hours a day for the next two weeks. You will not leave your home without parental supervision except to go to school or for any other like event that meets with parental approval. If there is any violation to this court order, you will immediately be returned to the custody of this court and return to juvenile hall." He looked over his half-rimmed glasses at Angela from his bench. "Do you understand what I just read to you?"

"Yes," she answered sheepishly.

"Do you agree to follow this court order?"

She agreed. We left the courtroom together. We hurried down the steps of the court building heading toward the parking lot. Angela squeezed my arm and squealed with delight.

"I'm free! I never want to go back to that place again!"

The following week there were tense moments, but I could see Angela was trying. A female government worker came to visit us as a part of the court-ordered home probation. I told her things were going well; however, the day after the lady left, Angela disappeared. When I couldn't find her, my emotions vacillated between fear and fury.

She strolled into the house two hours later.

"Where have you been?"

"I couldn't stand it any longer. I went to visit Chuck and lost track of time."

Farewell, My Free Bird

"You're not supposed to leave the house without permission. You were doing great until today. You're going to ruin it for yourself, Angela. This is no game. You either follow the rules or you send yourself back to juvenile hall!"

"It's no big deal that I went to Chuck's house!" She went up to her room and slammed the door.

The next day she calmly approached me. "Mom, I need to go to a Narcotics Anonymous meeting tonight. I've already called and talked to the lady who's in charge of the meeting."

Angela told me where the meeting was, what time it started and what time it ended. Wanting to get help and initiating it was a first for Angela, but should I trust her? I knew this would be considered a special circumstance by the court. If she was struggling with a desire to use drugs, attending the meeting would be good for her. Keith and I talked about it. We agreed to let her go to the meeting.

"You can go, but you'd better not violate our trust. You need to know we're not going to cover up for you if you're lying to us."

"I'm not lying to you. I really need to go."

I dropped her off at the meeting and waited until she went inside.

"Mom! Wait!" Angela ran to the car. "The lady in charge of the meeting said she would drive me home after the meeting."

"I don't know about that, Angela. I think I should pick you up."

"Mom, she's in charge of the meeting. I don't think you have to worry about her."

Hesitantly I agreed.

By eleven o'clock, I was furiously pacing the floors waiting for Angela, scolding myself for being so naive. Shortly after midnight, she came in the house wondering why I was awake and upset.

"Where have you been?" I demanded.

"Well, you don't have to get so mad. The lady took me to her house after the meeting and taught me how to play her guitar."

I came unglued, venting my built up frustrations.

"I expected you to be home no later than ten o'clock. I didn't know if something happened to you or if you ran away again. Don't you realize you're under a special court order?"

She kept insisting she did nothing wrong.

"For once in my life, I try to get help and what happens? I get in trouble."

"Angela, I'm going to bed. We'll talk about this in the morning."

It took a while before I could fall asleep. When I awoke in the morning, she was gone. Her bed had not been slept in. I had no choice. I reported her missing.

Two days later, an old pick-up truck, driven by a rough looking man in his thirties, pulled up in front of my sister and brother-in-law's home. Angela got out of the truck; the man quickly drove off.

Angela told them, "I met him the night I attended the N.A. meeting. He gave me his number and said if I ever needed a friend I could call him. Mom and I argued when I got home, so I called him and he picked me up at the end of our street. He took me to the canyons thirty miles away. I've been there with him for two days. He wouldn't let me leave. Finally, he agreed to drop me off at your house."

We were angry and horrified at the ramifications of what took place, if this was true. But none of us knew for sure what to believe.

Mary and Joe came with us for the next court hearing. With our permission, they requested Angela be released to them. But upon seeing the violations, the judge ordered Angela back to juvenile hall.

> *I just wish I was free as the winter's breeze . . .*
> *Just to do as I please,*
> *To sing as I want, to talk as I please,*
> *To sit by the water and near the trees,*
> *With a blue sky above me with blue birds as they sing,*
> *With the feeling now that I'm safe as can be,*
> *To think everything out very peacefully,*
> *I wish all of these things that I want to come true,*
> *But I guess it might be just another dream,*
> *That will make me blue.*
> *Angela, FREE BIRD*

Chapter Eight

I DO AS I PLEASE

"Then you will call upon me and come and pray to Me, and I will listen to you. You will seek Me and find me when you seek Me with all your heart. I will be found by you," declares the LORD, "and will bring you back from captivity . . ." (Jeremiah 29:12-14)

Angela spent the next two months in juvenile hall, and we set aside Sunday afternoons for our visits with her. We grew familiar with the tedious procedures necessary to get into the building.

Here, at juvenile hall, she was at her best. Her stay here helped Keith and I see the dynamics of her deep inner struggle. Without access to drugs, and in a structured environment with limited freedom, she seemed to thrive. The world with all its temptations was not easily accessible. She spoke once again of her desire to make it on the outside. She clearly saw her mistakes.

"This time it will be different," she told us.

We were hesitant to believe her, but we encouraged and challenged her when she spoke of her dream to be free.

I was learning to take one day at a time. We would see what the future held. Our Sunday afternoon visits became invaluable, forcing us to take time to talk of the deep hurts we both felt.

When we returned to court, Mary and Joe came with us. They still wanted to bring Angela home with them to live for a time. Angela agreed, and with mixed feelings we gave our consent. All of us expressed hope that *this* time it would be different.

It didn't take long for the judge to review her case. He decided to release her, but he ordered six months' probation. The courtroom was quiet. All of our attention was focused on the judge who sat silently; his eyes fixed on Angela. When he spoke, his voice boomed with authority and compassion. "Young lady, I see a lot of young people come in and out of this courtroom. You are not one who belongs in this judicial system. You have two parents who are here today who love you, and you have a future, a bright future, to look forward to if you choose to make the right choices. I don't want to see you here again, do you understand?"

"Yes, your honor," she replied.

We left the courtroom with Angela vowing once again never to return and intoxicated with the excitement of being free. We reminded her how important it was that she not violate probation, and if she did, we would not cover up or lie for her.

"I know and you don't have to worry. I'm not planning on violating it."

Mary and Joe enrolled Angela in a new high school. It worked well, for a time. At first, she made friends and did fairly well in school. We found a drug and alcohol treatment counselor in their area who met with Angela several times. We remained in close communication with Angela often bringing her home for the weekends.

By Christmas, Angela had been with Mary and Joe for three months.

We were cautiously optimistic that Angela was recovering; but, then, a few days before Christmas, Mary called. Angela was gone.

"She left the house last night and hasn't returned."

We had been through this so many times before; yet, my heart still raced with anxiety when I heard of her running away.

When the probation officer called, I sadly reported her missing.

I awoke Christmas morning exhausted. Anxiety for Angela's safety had made me restless and unable to sleep well. It had been three days since we had seen or heard from her.

Carl was in the military and unable to be home this Christmas. Keith, Travis, Jason, and I gathered around the tree to exchange gifts with one another. The few remaining gifts left unopened were another reminder to us that once again Angela was missing.

The phone rang. It was Mary. "Angela's here. She wants to be with the family today, but first she wants to be sure that you won't turn her in."

"Let me call you back."

Keith and I struggled with our decision, but our emotions overruled. We agreed Angela should be with us for Christmas. I hurried to the phone to tell Mary.

"Angela left," Mary said. "She decided not to wait for your call. She's really sick. She ran to the bathroom and vomited before she left the house. I don't know where she went."

As I hung up the phone, I thought of how lonely she must be feeling this Christmas day. The tremendous pain that *must* be unbearable for her; constantly running, but running from what?

Keith and I discussed with the boys that the court would no doubt return Angela to juvenile hall this time. The probation officer had already overlooked so many violations, giving Angela several chances to make it. The boys sometimes expressed anger at her behavior, and, sometimes, embarrassment. Often they felt bad for her, but now they had become so used to their sister being in trouble that they had learned to accept whatever new crisis arose.

I dressed for the day feeling overcome by waves of sadness. Yet, we needed to try to make the best of this holiday for the rest of the family. We loaded our car with gifts and drove to my parent's home for our traditional family gathering.

My mother expressed concern for Angela. "I don't know what it's going to take to reach her. I don't understand. She's wasting the best years of her life."

We each felt the effects; yet, we tried to enjoy the day. We elected Joe, *'Santa.'* As he handed out the gifts from under the Christmas tree, he would quietly tuck a present off to the side every once in a while. We all knew those were Angela's. Soon, the room was filled with a mass of torn wrapping paper and people expressing gratitude to each other for their gifts.

In the midst of our holiday celebration, Joe walked over to me. "Carol, Angela bought you a plant. It's outside. She came to the house with it this morning and asked us to make sure you got it. Do you want me to bring it in?"

"*No!*" My answer was quick and sharp. But Joe understood. He was also hurting. I was surprised and overwhelmed that amid her own turmoil, she bought me a gift. Holidays meant so much to Angela. Like a little child, she anticipated them with excitement. I smiled to myself as I thought of that special part of her that had remained intact.

The day ended. We gathered our gifts and the tray of food my mother insisted we take home with us.

"Don't forget your plant, Carol," my mother reminded me as we were leaving.

I walked out on the porch and saw it sitting there alone in the dark. I hesitated, feeling almost afraid to reach down for it. I picked it up carefully and carried it in my arms to the car. Travis and Jason chatted in the back seat while we drove home. I held Angela's gift on my lap watering the lush green leaves with my tears. Keith reached over and squeezed my hand.

Ten days had passed and not a word from Angela. With each day our fears mounted. Was she so afraid of returning to juvenile hall that she decided to leave and never return? Worse yet, had something happened to her?

Finally, my sister called me, "I just talked with Angela on the phone."

Thank God, I thought, *she's alive!*

"She's in Arizona," Mary said.

I was stunned! She had never left the state before.

"She said she drove to Phoenix with some guys. They promised her if she went with them they would pay her way back whenever she was ready to return. Now, they won't let her leave. She made an excuse to go to the laundromat and called me from there. She's broke and wants us to help her."

My head was spinning. We had to do something!

"Mary, did she give you any other information, a phone number, or an address?"

"I have the phone number of the laundromat. She's going to be there at five tomorrow night. She wants me to call her then."

"That might be enough to go on. I'm going to call the Phoenix Police Department and see if they'll pick her up. I'm sure with this phone number they can locate the laundromat and be there when she arrives tomorrow."

For a few seconds Mary was quiet. "She'll think I betrayed her. I promised her she could trust me."

"Mary, we don't know who these guys are she's with or why they took her to Arizona. She may be in danger. We have to get her back here."

"They'll send her back to juvenile hall. Being in juvenile hall hasn't helped her. It's just made things worse."

"She's violated probation. She probably will be sent back, but she'll be safer there than where she is now. We have no choice."

Mary gave me the phone number. I called the Phoenix Police Department and gave them the information, hoping they would follow through and be there to pick her up. *O Lord, don't let anything go wrong. Please bring her home safely.* The next day seemed like an eternity as the hours slowly passed. Finally, I received the call I had been waiting for.

"Mrs. Noe, this is the Phoenix Police Department; we have your daughter Angela in our custody."

> *I belong to myself,*
> *And I am free as a bird.*
> *I fly through whatever I want,*
> *I have no one to answer to.*
> *I do as I please,*
> *I am on a never-ending breeze.*
> *Angela, FREE BIRD*

Chapter Nine

MIXED FEELINGS

"When anxiety was great within me, Your consolation brought joy to my soul." (Psalm 94:19)

A Phoenix police officer handcuffed Angela and put her on a plane. A Los Angeles County deputy sheriff waited to meet her at LAX and drive her directly to juvenile hall.

We saw Angela for the first time in the courtroom. She sat next to the public defender. Her eyes darted from us to the judge, uncertain of what would take place. This time the public defender hadn't tried to convince or persuade us to intervene. There were no options. Angela would return to juvenile hall, but for how long we didn't know.

The judge spoke, "You have violated this court order by breaking probation and leaving the state of California. You will be detained in juvenile hall for the next six months."

Angela stared in disbelief. She looked helplessly to the public defender, appealing for his help. He shook his head and communicated to her that there was nothing he could do. My intense feelings of relief puzzled me. I wanted her in a safe place, even if it meant juvenile hall. How much longer could she survive abusing drugs and alcohol while deliberately placing herself in dangerous circumstances? But I also realized how much I dreaded Angela's return home. I hurt for her, but we had lived in turmoil for so long. I didn't know how much more I could take of the arguments, the lies, the rebellion, and the running away. No matter what her resolve, it never lasted. How many more disappointments were there going to be? How many more times would we have to worry where she was and wonder if she was alive or dead? Maybe this six-month stay would break the pattern of destruction. The district attorney told Keith and me that we could visit Angela before we left the courthouse. We followed a guard into a small, cramped room. We sat on the unsteady plastic chairs staring at the thick clear glass in front of us. A door opened on the other side. Angela entered the tiny room and sat down.

She hesitantly smiled at us. "Hi, Mom and Dad."

"It's hard to hear you through this glass," I said.

She raised her voice, "Thanks for being here." She paused. "I've never told you this before, but I realize you've always been there for me. I've never appreciated it before, but I do now."

It sounded good. I wanted to believe her, but my guard automatically went up.

"I don't want to go back to juvenile hall. I know I did this to myself. I'm going to try to do my best while I'm there."

"It sounds good, Angela. I hope you mean it."

"You'll see. I'm going to make it."

The guard opened the door and motioned for her to leave.

"Bye Mom! Bye Dad! I love you."

We raised our voices so she could hear us, "Bye Angela. We love you too."

"Come and see me on Sunday, okay?"

We nodded; she disappeared behind the closed door.

We saw her at juvenile hall on Sunday. We were welcomed with a warm hug. She snuggled close to me while we visited, often resting her head on my shoulder. She reminded us of her appreciation for us.

"Mom," she asked, "Did you get the plant I bought you for Christmas?"

"I did, and I love it. Thank you for thinking of me."

She told us, "That was the most miserable Christmas I've ever spent! I had the flu. I felt so bad that I'd blown it. I wanted to be with the family. Instead, I drank alcohol all day. I had to keep running to the bathroom every few minutes to be sick. The next day, two guys asked me to drive to Arizona with them. I figured why not? They promised me I could come back whenever I wanted to."

She tightened her grip on my arm.

"One of the men had a gun and threatened to kill me. I realized they were not going to let me come back home. One night they let me take a walk. I was half-stoned and wondering what to do. I fell on the grass, and prayed that God would make Himself real to me. I did feel His presence, and I asked Him to help me get out of this mess. He did. And I'm here. The night I didn't return to the motel, they probably thought I snitched on them, and they are probably trying to find me."

Our visits with her remained positive. I sensed she was sincere. I struggled with expectations. I tried not to hope for too much because it hurt to be disappointed. Yet, why would she be manipulating Keith or me? She had already been sentenced, and we could do nothing to change it.

One afternoon, she spoke to us again of her heart's desire. "This time I'm going to make it and get my life together. And when I get out of here I want to help other teenagers who are going through what I'm going through."

We encouraged her. Angela always cared for others. She possessed the strength, the determination, and the personality to effectively make a difference in others' lives if she only *could* make it and get her life together. Her determination to do things *her way,* along with her addictions, had made her a selfish and defeated person. Maybe she was beginning to see that now.

A month later, Angela was ecstatic when her probation officer told her she could leave juvenile hall to go into placement. She would stay in Hollywood at a huge, old, two-story house, made over into a state facility for juvenile girls. It sat up on a hill. Its spacious, antique rooms and its homey atmosphere were impressive. Their program was set up like the hospital Angela had stayed in previously. If the girls did well, their reward was more freedom. It was a locked facility, yet a few of the girls had earned the privilege of attending the neighborhood high school and some even had part-time jobs while living at the home.

Angela was enthusiastic. "I've always wanted to live in Hollywood!" she said dreamily.

After living in this placement in Hollywood for a short time, she exclaimed, "Everything is working out absolutely wonderful! I like it here. I've made friends with the girls, and the staff is friendly to us. They treat us like human beings. It's nothing like juvenile hall."

The three of us met at the home each week for counseling. Angela did well the first month, but she wasn't progressing like she should. She wanted the freedom, but her resistance to keeping the rules kept her from gaining extra privileges. She barely maintained her school grades. She complained to us about her teacher.

"I know she doesn't like me, and I don't like her. She picks on me no matter what I do. Even if I'm trying, I get in trouble."

After causing daily disruptions in the classroom, cursing the teacher, and making excuses for not turning her work in, the staff refused to let her attend the classroom.

Six weeks after Angela had been in the home, she ran away with a friend. I don't know why, but it surprised me that she ran from this court-ordered placement. The following day, she called me.

"Will you pick me up? I didn't intend to run away," she said. "My friend asked me to help her get over the wall. I tried to talk her out of it, but she wouldn't listen. So I agreed to help her. Someone saw us and started yelling to the staff that we were running away. I knew I was already in trouble, so I went over the wall with her."

"Oh! Angela! The probation officer worked so hard to get you into this place. He was trying to give you a chance. Don't you see? You weren't helping that girl, and now you've gotten yourself into trouble. Do you realize how serious this is?"

I returned her to the home. We parked in front. "You know they may not let you come back. You may be going back to juvenile hall today."

We knocked on the door and waited.

"Well, look who we have here," the lady said. She let us in, and we followed her into her tiny office. The lady winked at me when Angela wasn't looking. Angela started talking fast, explaining the circumstances.

"So, do you think that's going to change my mind?" The lady continued to reprimand her. "Angela, there's really no reason why I should take you back."

For several minutes Angela stood in front of her listening politely and nervously waiting for the final decision.

"I really shouldn't give you another chance," the lady said, "but if you promise me you'll try and work hard in school and do what you're supposed to, I'll let you stay. But, you'd better not run again."

Angela looked like she had been through a war and won. Her worried face broke into a smile. "I'll try. I promise you I'll try."

I left breathing a sigh of relief. *Thank you Lord!*

The staff took her to a doctor to be treated for a vaginal infection. He informed us that Angela had infectious gonorrhea and syphilis. She had gone untreated for too long. The infections had done their damage. Internal tissues were destroyed. After the examination and test results, the doctor gave Angela the devastating news. She would never be able to bear a child due to the irreparable damage that had been done to her body.

Angela expressed disappointment, but didn't appear extremely disturbed by it. Someday, I thought, this is going to hit her hard. Someday, she's going to grieve over this loss.

Once again, she set out to follow the rules at the placement, and she earned the privilege to come home for the day. Paula came to visit her. The girls spent valuable hours together recapturing the time lost from months of being apart. Angela enjoyed being home, but this time there was an aura of sadness about her. She resolutely picked up her purse and said goodbye when it was time to leave. Her visit home was a painful reminder to her and to us how unnatural things had become. If only it could work. If only it could be different. The drive back to the home was quiet.

"Angela, you only have three more months to go before you can come home. You've got to hang in there and make the right choices. Before you know it, your time will be up, and I'll be picking you up to take you home for good!"

"Yeah, I know."

Three weeks later, they found her and her friend smoking marijuana in their room. They generously gave her another chance.

Keith went to visit her on a Sunday afternoon. He returned home concerned that she would run again.

"We talked for over an hour," Keith said. "She was moody and extremely sad. I just didn't feel right about her when I left. I'm afraid she's going to take off again."

That night we received the call. A few hours after Keith left, she had disappeared over the wall.

"Damn!" Keith shouted. He slammed his hand on the table. "I knew something like this was going to happen. Why can't she just do what she's supposed to? Why does she keep messing up her life?"

I wondered if this time Angela would decide not to contact us, knowing she would be returning to juvenile hall.

A few days later, on a Saturday, I half-heartedly dressed for a Mother's Day luncheon. I had committed to be part of a fashion show, but my heart wasn't in it. As I finished getting ready, the phone rang.

The lady on the phone identified herself as Nancy, a counselor at an adolescent drug program. The home Angela stayed in had brought the girls to the meetings she held, and she and Angela had met there. Angela was with her now, she said, and I could meet them at the home. I left immediately and found them both waiting in the parking lot.

Nancy came over to the car. "Angela spent the night with me last night. She agreed to turn herself in. They're probably not going to let her back in the home, but I thought I'd give it a try anyway."

The three of us went in together. Nancy appealed to them to give Angela another chance, but they refused.

"You need to drive her to juvenile hall. I'll let them know you're on your way," the lady at the home said firmly.

We filled the trunk and the back seat of the car with Angela's belongings.

"Why did you run?" I asked.

"I just couldn't take it anymore!"

"Yes, but look where it got you."

"I know, but it's too late now."

As we drove toward the freeway, I noticed her anxiously looking out the window.

"What's wrong, Angela?"

She didn't answer me until we were on the freeway. Then, she told me about her means of survival the first two nights after leaving the home.

"Mom, you're not going to like what I have to say. I was depressed. I didn't think I could take another day at the home. I left without thinking how I was going to make it or what I'd do. The first night, a man came up to me and offered me a place to stay if I worked for him."

"You mean prostitution?"

"Yeah . . . . After the second night, I realized he was just using me, so I disappeared with some of his money. If he ever sees me again, he'll kill me."

My mind went crazy with thoughts of the dangerous situation she allowed herself to be in and of her prostituting herself with a multitude of strange men, and how this man used her like an object for his personal gain.

"Angela. Why? Don't you know you're worth so much more than that?"

"Mom, I don't want to talk about it right now. Remember, I didn't have to tell you. Anyway, I called Nancy to pick me up. She convinced me to be honest with you and to turn myself in."

Farewell, My Free Bird

"You're doing the right thing by turning yourself in. It will be hard for you to go back, but in another few months you'll be out if you follow the rules, no matter how you feel."

"I know tomorrow is Mother's Day. I wanted so badly to go to a flower shop and send you flowers, but it didn't work out. I'm sorry. Now, I don't have any gift for you."

"Angela, just knowing that you are safe right now and being honest with me is the best gift you can give me."

We checked in at the desk.

A male guard came over to us. "Well, say goodbye to your mother. It's time to go."

I watched while he took her down the hall. She turned and waved to me before she disappeared around the corner.

"Happy Mother's Day! I love you!"

You see as they walk on by wanting to scream,
And helpless tears in their eyes,
Nowhere to go . . . nowhere to turn.
Never know love, only how to hate.
As they wait in the streets wanting your love,
You slap them away because you say you see it every day.
This is a world of hate . . . a continued debate.
Mixed feelings flowing through our heads,
We would much rather be dead.
But we just hold our heads up high as we walk on by.
We can't show our hurt, things would only get worse.
We're juvenile delinquents and have no say,
So we walk the streets day after day.
Angela, FREE BIRD

Chapter Ten

NEVER AGAIN

"Restore to me the joy of Your salvation and grant me a willing spirit, to sustain me." (Psalm 51:12)

Oscar, Angela's probation officer, had worked hard to get her into placement. Now that she had run from the home again, he said there was no other choice but to double her six-month sentence. She had looked forward to coming home in two months, but now it would be longer.

"We'll see how she does. If she cooperates in juvenile hall, I'll try to place her again."

It overwhelmed Angela to think of spending additional time in the hall. She cried and complained for weeks. She was angry at the system and angry at herself. She begged us to try to get her out. Finally, she accepted the inevitable.

When Oscar was convinced that Angela had learned from her past mistakes at the home and saw she was cooperating in the hall, he told us of his plans.

"I've applied for Angela to be admitted into a new placement. It won't be easy to get her into this one. This home is very selective. It's one of the finest alcohol and drug rehabs available, but it's also one of the strictest."

Angela's eagerness to be placed again turned to indignation when she heard she would have to be interviewed by a staff member from the home.

"So, what if I don't say what they want to hear. I don't like people playing games with me. Either they want me in their program or they don't."

We feared she'd be stubborn and ruin it for herself. Keith and I held our breath the day of the interview. We waited in suspense for several days before hearing the results.

Oscar called us, and with relief evident in his voice he told us, "They accepted her!"

The following day, Oscar drove her to her new residence. Angela called us, her speech enthusiastic and rapid.

"I only have a few minutes to talk to you. Bring all my things from home. I can have my radio and my own bedspread and posters. Mom, bring everything! I'll see you when you get here."

I loaded the car with as many things as I thought she could have and drove the forty-five miles to see her.

I found the white one-story building on the corner of a busy street. I walked through the entrance, my arms loaded with bags of clothing. A young, bearded man working at the front desk had his head buried in paper work.

"My daughter, Angela Noe, was admitted here today," I said while interrupting his concentration. "I'm her mother."

He stood up and walked from behind the desk. "Just set her things on the floor, and I'll go through them."

After making several trips to unload the car, I asked to see Angela.

"I'm sorry, you can't see her. Our new residents can't have visitors the first two weeks they're here. That includes parents."

I was disappointed, but impressed with their uncompromising rules.

Two weeks later, Angela called bubbling over with positive reports about this wonderful, new placement. Of course, she had lots of new friends! Oscar gave me permission to take her to our dentist, so I picked her up, looking forward to the short time we would have together.

She rushed eagerly into the waiting room to greet me. I received a big hug and her smile conveyed life was good for her now. A girl stood next to her.

"Mom, this is Laura!"

"Hi, Laura." She was tall and slender, a picture of innocence. She smiled warmly and giggled while Angela explained her presence.

"She's my big sister while I'm here. We share a room together. Everywhere I go she goes with me, so she has to go with us today."

I was surprised, but it probably was a good idea. So often our times together turned from light and fun to stress-filled moments when Angela didn't get her own way. Having her friend along might prevent this from happening.

When we arrived at the dentist's office, we were met by a very frustrated dentist. He had put Angela's braces on over two years ago. Her absence for so many appointments meant there had been little progress.

"She must keep her appointments, or we are wasting our time. We might as well just take them off if she doesn't come in when she's supposed to."

On the way back, we stopped to have lunch.

"Mom, you look 'mod' today."

"Thanks." Usually I looked too old fashioned for her approval. It made her feel good if I dressed in what she considered stylish. In times past, she fixed my hair to her liking. I would modify it somewhat, by combing down the heavily sprayed teased hair. Her wild attempts at spiking my hair would cause me to laugh. Compliments from Angela were rare, but precious, to me.

It had been a delightful afternoon. After that first visit with her, Keith and I saw her weekly. Angela's self-esteem improved. This time, she willingly participated in the group therapy.

One evening during one of our counseling sessions, she told us, "I've been embarrassed to talk about my life out on the streets. Some of the things that happened to me, I didn't want others to know about. Besides, I didn't think the teenagers in my group would understand. My therapist encouraged me to be honest. The other night in our group session, I talked about my life on the street, and they still accepted me!"

It was a breakthrough for Angela. Weeks later, she initiated a conversation with Keith and me, telling us what she learned from working the twelve steps. Her hesitation and her unsteady voice let us know that what she wanted to say was important but difficult for her.

"Now that I'm going through this program, I realize how important it is to make amends. I'm sorry for what I've put you both through. I hope things can be different."

We never thought we would hear these cherished words. It meant a lot to us. I saw her determination to make it right. We assured her of our love and encouraged her that things could be different.

It was August. Angela had been in this placement for six weeks when we reluctantly told her of our plans to leave on a three-week family vacation. Keith and I knew how hard it would be for Angela to accept that this time she wouldn't be going with us. As we expected, the news upset her. The night before we left on our trip, Keith and I met with Angela and her therapist. We brought in pizza. The four of us sat around the table eating, when Angela told Keith of her most recent fears.

"Dad, I've been afraid lately that something is going to happen to you. I'm just beginning to understand how important you and Mom are to me. What if the whole family gets in an accident while you're on the trip? I wouldn't be able to stand it if anything happened."

She had never worried about us like this before. We tried to console her. We said goodbye to her, promising that we would call her when we got there.

A few days later, we arrived at Keith's parents' home in Kansas. With the excitement of arriving and greeting relatives, I didn't call her immediately. I felt extremely guilty when I talked to her on the phone and heard her anxious, almost panicked, voice. "I thought something happened to you!"

"We're alright, Angela," I assured her.

We talked for several minutes before saying goodbye.

"I miss you guys so much. I can hardly wait until you come home."

I wrote a letter, hoping my communication would make it easier for her. The following week, I felt an unexplainable heaviness whenever I thought of Angela. I sensed she was struggling. One morning, after awakening, I prayed for Angela. I spent time reading the Scriptures, and again, the words came alive when I read verses in Isaiah. I heard an inaudible voice convey words to me that were promises for Angela. As I read Isaiah 40:28-31, I felt a peace and a new hope settle within.

> *"Do you not know? Have you not heard? The Lord is the everlasting God, the Creator of the ends of the earth. He will not grow tired or weary, and His understanding no one can fathom. He gives strength to the weary and*

increases the power of the weak. Even youths grow tired and weary, and young men stumble and fall; but those who hope in the Lord will renew their strength. They will soar on wings like eagles; they will run and not grow weary, they will walk and not be faint."

The heaviness that had been there vanished as quickly and as strangely as it had appeared. I continued praying for Angela, knowing God cared for her, knowing that He loved her more than I ever could as a mother. I could trust God to take care of her.

Our vacation went by quickly. We left Keith's folks' home on Saturday morning before daybreak, thankful for the rest and enjoyment we had experienced. I looked forward to seeing Angela and being home again.

Janice, a friend of ours, had volunteered to house-sit for us while we were gone. When we checked into a motel, I went to the phone booth to call Janice and tell her we were on our way home.

"Carol, I'm so glad you called! I've been trying to reach you. Angela's probation officer called this morning. Angela cut her arms with a razor blade last night."

"Is she alright?"

"Oscar said it wasn't serious enough to take her in for treatment. She's back in juvenile hall right now. That's all I know, Carol. I'm sorry."

I stood outside the phone booth fighting tears. Feelings of disappointment, hopelessness, sadness for Angela, confusion, and guilt for going on vacation overpowered me. I glanced at our motel room that now seemed so distant. I walked by the people sitting by the pool, hoping I could get to the room before losing control of my emotions. Keith and the boys looked up when I came into the room.

Keith asked, "Is something wrong?"

They listened while I told them what had happened.

"She didn't need any medical treatment, so her wounds aren't critical."

We each felt perplexed and helpless. We headed for home and turned into our driveway Sunday evening, still racing with anxiety from the upsetting turn of events.

Early Monday morning, I called Oscar.

"Her cuts were superficial. She sketched designs in her arms with a razor blade. The placement didn't want to deal with that kind of behavior. They decided to send her back to juvenile hall."

"How is she handling this?"

"I've heard she's not handling it very well. I have an appointment to meet with her this afternoon. I can make special arrangements to get you in, if you and your husband want to see her today."

We met Oscar outside the building. He led us into a small room. The three of us sat waiting for the guard to bring Angela into the room.

She opened the door and saw Oscar first. She walked in as if in a daze. She looked pale; her eyes were red. When she saw us, she expressed shock, then relief.

"You're back!" She ran over and hugged us. She wept in my arms. I led her to a chair next to us. She hung on to my arm while trying to speak. Her words were barely coherent. She sobbed uncontrollably.

"I've been crying ever since I got here. I can't stop. I don't know what's the matter with me. I've been so depressed. I couldn't stand you being gone. I tried. But it got to be too much. I couldn't handle it any longer. I liked it there, and I was doing so well. I begged them to give me another chance, but they wouldn't. I don't know if I can take it anymore. I'm not a bad person. I shouldn't be locked up." Tears streamed down her face. "I don't want to stay here any longer. I can't!" I held her while she cried.

Oscar interrupted us saying she needed to return. Angela clung to me.

"Come back Sunday," she pleaded with us.

I answered, "We'll be here, Angela. We love you, and we're praying for you."

As soon as I got home, I wrote her a letter of encouragement. All week, thoughts of her consumed me. She looked so pathetic and so desperately hurt. In Friday's mail, I received a letter from her.

> Mom and Dad,
> I was really a mess the day you came to see me, but ever since Monday I've been doing a lot better. I know I shouldn't have cut myself. Now, I'll just have to wait out my time here in the hall and make the best of it. I love you. See you Sunday.
> Love, Angela

When Angela had only a few months left to serve, Jason, our youngest son, started writing encouraging letters to his sister. He gave very wise advice for a twelve year old, telling her he loved her and believed in her. He included Scripture for her to read and reminded her of his prayers for her. Touched by his letters, she responded warmly, telling him the positive plans she had for her future. She asked him to continue praying for her.

Oscar gave me permission once again to take her to the dentist. This time, Oscar arranged for us to have a six-hour pass. We quickly took care of the dentist appointment and hurried home to spend the rest of the day there. Angela was so happy to be home and to see her brothers again. It had been so long. Jason and she had a lot to talk about. Angela called me into the bathroom to show me the new hair style she had created for Jason.

"Doesn't he look cute?"

I could hardly say he looked cute with his heavily sprayed spiked hair. I could only laugh at the sight.

"It's not so bad, Mom," Jason said, trying not to hurt her feelings.

Angela and I made cookies. Oscar stopped by the house to bring the rest of Angela's clothes that had been left at the last placement.

Angela presented him with a plate of cookies, "Here, Oscar, these are the best chocolate chip cookies you'll ever eat!"

He smiled. "I'm sure they will be. Well, I have to leave. Enjoy your day."

After dinner, I drove Angela back to juvenile hall.

"This was fun. It was good to be home," Angela said. "I can hardly wait until the day I'm finally free."

That day finally came in December, three weeks before Christmas.

With mixed feelings I drove to juvenile hall to bring Angela home. Oscar met me there.

"Well, this is the big day." I said to him.

Oscar looked at me, his face serious. "I don't want to tell you there's no Santa Claus but . . ." Then he stopped. "Good luck."

Angela came through the door with a guard, her face beaming with excitement.

"Mom, I'm free! I'm free!" She carried a bag in her hands containing a change of clothes, and the few personal belongings she kept while in the hall. "Let's go home!"

> *Never again will I wanna feel lonely,*
> *Never again will I smoke a stogy,*
> *Never again will I lower myself.*
> *That's not life . . . No it's not for me.*
> *Keep it <u>far</u> from me.*
> *Oh God please never bring it back.*
> *For if it shall ever come to pass it will surely not last.*
> *For I will die before there is no respect and druggie in me.*
> *For this is the truth for you all to see.*
> *Never again shall I see you hurt . . . as well as me.*
> *Angela, FREE BIRD*

Chapter Eleven

CRYING IN THE MIDDLE OF THE NIGHT

"Hear my prayer, O LORD, listen to my cry for help; be not deaf to my weeping." (Psalm 39:12)

As Angela unpacked her things, she held up her thirty-day ribbon for me to see.

"I earned it in the twelve step program for being alcohol free for thirty days. I would've gotten my sixty day ribbon too, if I didn't have to go back to juvenile hall." She proudly displayed her ribbon on the wall. "This will help me remember that I can do it."

She called Paula and within minutes they were together.

"Can Paula and I go for a walk? We won't be long."

"Sure but we have to leave the house in half an hour."

Forty-five minutes had passed, and Angela hadn't returned.

Keith was furious. "Here we go again! Her first night home and she's gone."

"I don't think she's going to take off the first night she's home."

I tried to reassure him, but I was worried too.

"Let's get in the car and look for her."

We drove to the end of the street and saw the girls. Angela ran to the car.

"Sorry. I thought I'd be on time." She laughed as she said goodbye to Paula. She was totally unaware of how fearful we had been. Keith and I glanced at each other sighing with relief. We needed to relax and not panic so easily. We drove off listening to her delight in the simple things, like having the freedom to take a walk. Disagreements surfaced, but we made an effort to keep our communication open, knowing how vital it would be. But with each day she became more easily irritated. She often couldn't sleep and would be up till the early morning hours.

Things continued getting shaky, but on Christmas morning I awakened feeling satisfied that this Christmas Angela was home and she was safe. After our family time Christmas morning, we left for my parents to spend the rest of our Christmas day with family there.

Angela was delighted that her cousin Lisa was there with her newborn baby girl. It was a heartfelt moment that day when I watched Angela holding the baby in her arms. Angela smiled and talked quietly to her. Then, her countenance changed. Her smile faded, and her face became solemn. I wondered if she was feeling the impact of the doctor's words: *"You'll never be able to bear a child."* I wondered if this was the first time she felt the full impact of those words.

An ever-increasing downward spiral continued after Christmas. Angela was discontented with almost everything. She was testing our patience and determined to do things her way. She and I had an argument, and, in my anger and frustration, I asked her to leave.

Farewell, My Free Bird

In the days to follow, my emotions were like a yo-yo: one moment enjoying the peace in our home, the next, worrying about Angela. I felt guilty that once again things had not worked out.

Angela was seventeen and would be eighteen years old in three months. One morning, feeling overwhelmed at all the crises that could still be ahead for Angela, and for our family, I clearly heard God speak to me once again. He didn't speak in an audible voice; nevertheless, I heard Him say, *"Carol, can you handle right now? Can you handle this moment?"*

Yes, Lord, I can handle right now.

He spoke again, *"Carol, I'll be there for all your tomorrows and each day you will always have enough grace for the moment."* With that I felt peace and a renewed strength to go on.

Angela called occasionally to talk with me as if nothing had happened between us. A motel in Pomona, California, was her new residence, she said.

It was a dangerous place for her to be. A few nights later, my sister, Mary, called. We had thought Angela might be prostituting herself. After discussing our fears for her, our emotions overruled. We decided to find her and try to reason with her. I knew God had impressed upon me not to rescue her or enable her anymore, but I had to try just one more time.

I told Keith of our plan, and he responded, "You're wasting your time going up there. I don't like the idea, but I guess if you feel you have to do it, I can't stop you."

Before I left, I took Keith's police badge and dropped it in my purse.

We left Mary's house in her new car, knowing Angela wouldn't recognize it. It was late at night. We drove to Pomona through the seediest part of town looking for the motel Angela had mentioned. Mary dimmed the car lights as we turned into the parking lot. As we slowly drove past each room, I tried to catch a glimpse of Angela through the gap in the curtains.

"I see her! She's in there!" I called out.

"Are you sure it's her?"

The cheap curtains hung unevenly and through the small opening I saw her standing in front of a mirror, combing her hair.

"It looks like she's getting ready to go somewhere. She's dressed up, and now she's putting makeup on."

We parked the car.

But before we could get out of the car, Angela's door opened. Angela, and an African-American man who looked to be in his mid-twenties, climbed into a small red pickup truck. I heard her laughing at something he had said. They pulled out of the parking lot in a hurry and onto the boulevard. We were soon trailing behind them, hoping the driver wouldn't notice he was being followed. I looked for signs of her being forced or afraid. Angela's body moved in rhythm as if listening to music. I felt an enormous pit in my stomach as I watched them conversing and I saw her laugh.

We nearly lost them at the intersection, but Mary sped through the red light. The truck increased its speed. Had they noticed us following them? The vehicle abruptly turned left into another motel. We continued straight ahead, and then turned the car around only to see him leaving in the red truck alone. We had lost sight of Angela! He must have dropped her off at one of these rooms.

"But if they saw us following them," I said, "it could be a trick to throw us off. She might have been hiding in the truck."

Not being sure what to do, we pulled into a vacant parking lot across the street facing the motel. We kept our eyes fixed on the shabby motel.

"What if she's in one of those rooms?" I asked.

One of the porch lights was on. Was that her signal? Should we call the police? But what if we were mistaken? We decided to wait.

This man was her pimp! I knew there had been many incidences of prostitution before, but to be faced with it as I was tonight was crushing. It seemed like an eternity sitting there waiting, knowing that Angela might be in one of these motel rooms prostituting herself with a stranger.

"How could she degrade herself like this?" Mary asked.

We shared our hurt and disappointment, and our feelings of being overwhelmed, not understanding why Angela would choose this for herself. Why was she so set on self-destruction?

We were in the worst part of town. While keeping our eyes on the motel, we cautiously watched our surroundings. Occasionally, someone would drive by on the boulevard and slow down as they noticed us in our parked car. With our car doors locked and the key in the ignition, we were ready to leave in a hurry if needed. A police officer would be a welcome sight.

"Mary, does Joe know where you are?"

"I left a note on the table." My brother-in law would have gotten home from work a few hours ago.

"He's probably worried. I told him what we were going to do." Mary said.

After a grueling ninety minutes, we determined we must have somehow missed Angela. Feeling discouraged, we decided to head back out on the boulevard and return to the first motel. We drove just a few blocks before we saw the red truck turn onto a side street that would lead to the street behind the motel.

"Mary, it's him! He's by himself!"

We followed. I saw a figure standing in the dark. It was Angela. She was waiting for him.

As Angela climbed into his truck, Mary drove her car into an empty lot to turn around. He looked in our direction, and then quickly drove his truck toward us. He positioned his vehicle across the exit so we were hemmed in. He jumped out of his truck and rushed toward us.

"Oh my God! What do we do?"

"Get out of here any way you can!" I answered.

"What about Angela?"

"We've got to get out of here and find the police!"

Mary stepped on the gas. She barely made it around him and his truck, driving over the curb, and out onto the street. He ran back to his truck, and soon he was tail-gaiting us.

"Mary, stay on the boulevard. I'll watch for a police car."

Suddenly, I couldn't believe what I was seeing! There was my brother-in-law, Joe, in his car looking for us. Realizing the danger we were in, he positioned himself behind the red truck, distracting the guy from us. The guy turned off onto a side street and Joe followed. We headed for the police station.

A few blocks from the station, we saw a police car and frantically motioned for the officers to pull over. Suspicious of us stopping them in the early morning hours in such a panic, they shined their bright lights into our car. One of the police officers cautiously approached us, while the other stood behind our vehicle.

"What seems to be the problem, ladies?"

"We need help!" I took a deep breath. My heart was beating rapidly. I could hardly get the words out. I held up Keith's police badge that I had taken off his uniform before I left the house, just in case I got into this kind of mess.

"My husband is a police officer."

Farewell, My Free Bird

He looked surprised. He listened while I told him what had happened.

"Lady, this is a dangerous place to be, especially this time of night."

They agreed to follow us to the first motel. If Joe or Angela were not there, then they would look for them. As we neared the motel, we could see Joe standing by his parked car. The police quickly pulled in front of us and jumped out of their patrol car.

"This is my brother-in-law!" I told the police officers.

Joe motioned to the motel room. "They're in there. But, you're wasting your time. This is what she wants to do. Angela told the guy I was her uncle. He pulled over and let her out of the truck to talk to me. She says that's her guy! He takes care of her." He shook his head. "She's doing what she wants to do."

We listened in disbelief.

The officer spoke very kindly to me, "From our experience, ma'am, unless she wants to leave, it won't do you any good to force her."

I knew I was grasping at straws. "Do you think she might be afraid of this guy? Could you arrange for us to talk to her alone?"

"Sure. We'll check this guy for warrants. If he has any, we'll take him in. If not, we'll detain him until you have a chance to talk to your daughter."

We stood back while they banged on the door.

"Police Officers! Open the door!"

The door slowly opened.

"Step outside!"

Angela and this man stood outside. The officers checked him for weapons. He did have an outstanding warrant. They handcuffed him and put him in the back seat of their car. As they drove off with him, I watched Angela's eyes meet his. She seemed heartbroken. She looked like she had lost her best friend. She smiled and waved, and he waved back.

We followed her into her dingy motel room. She sat on the bed and lit up a cigarette. She was obviously disgusted with us.

"Who do you think you are coming here and interfering with my life? Look what you've done! You had him arrested!"

"Why should you care if he's arrested? He doesn't care about you. If he did he wouldn't be using you like he is!"

"I want you to leave me alone, and let me live my life the way I want."

Joe, Mary, and I, stood in the room with Angela, trying to reason with her.

"Angela," I said, "You don't need to live like this."

"Leave me alone. I'm doing what I want to. Everything was fine until you interfered."

"Why don't you come to our house tonight?" Mary asked.

"No. I'm going to stay here."

"Then, come to my house tomorrow when you leave here."

"I'll think about it."

We left her sitting on the bed. She appeared to be under the influence of something. Her eyes were glazed, and she looked hard and pathetic.

Before we got into the car, Mary said, "I have to try one more time."

"Go ahead. I'm going to wait here."

Joe walked over.

"I guess I'll have to let her go." I said.

"I don't think anyone is going to be able to reach her, Carol."

I felt numb. I couldn't even cry. I couldn't feel anything.

Mary returned to the car. "She won't listen."

We drove back to their house in silence. It was too much to absorb for one night. Everyone was sleeping when I arrived home. My mind raced with troubling thoughts of what had taken place. Why would Angela choose the streets, instead of being here with us? Why would she refuse the help we were willing to give her?

I recalled a conversation I had with Shawn, our pastor.

He said, "When Angela got out of juvenile hall, she told me that prostitution was not an option for her anymore. She would rather die than go back into that."

That was just a few months ago. What had happened in such a short time? What kind of force was driving her? The pain she must be in. I got on my knees. *God, help her! Let her know how special she is. Let her know she doesn't need to live like this.* God had made it clear to me before tonight that I was to let go of her and trust Him with her. *I'm sorry, Lord. I just had to try one more time.*

I sensed a gentle spirit speak within, *"Carol, now will you let go?"*

Yes, Lord. I can let her go now.

I accepted how very helpless I was. I said what I could never say before, *God, if you know that she'll never be able to get out of this, then for the very first time, I understand if you choose to take her home.* The dam burst, and the frozen tears came like a flood.

> *Yea, she is a whore on the street that everyone meets,*
> *And you'll be crying for more.*
> *She's a bitch if you ever wanta snitch,*
> *And she'll tear you apart.*
> *Yea, she knows no love only how to hate.*
> *If you want her you'll surely get laid.*

But she wishes she could tear it all away.
Yea, she's been through it all.
What more could she take, she's a one night stand,
And she'll take what she can.
But can't you hear her crying in the middle of the night,
Wishing for love, but there's no tears in sight.
                              Angela, FREE BIRD

Chapter Twelve

I JUST WANT TO BE FREE TO BE ME

"Then you will call, and the LORD will answer; you will cry for help, and He will say: Here am I." (Isaiah 58:9)

The next morning Angela called. "Look what you've done. My friend is in jail because of you. Just wait! When he gets out, we're going to get married. You'll never see me again!"

I waited until she finished venting her anger.

"Are you through, Angela?" She gave no reply.

"You don't have to worry. I'll never do anything like that again. From now on you're on your own. You can live your life any way you want to without my interference. But, don't call and expect me to rescue you, either."

"That's what you say, but I don't trust you. Maybe you'll never hear from me again."

With that she slammed the receiver down.

The thought of not hearing from her for a while was almost a relief. But, it was only a few weeks before she started calling again, just to talk and keep in touch. She lived in a different motel. I didn't bother to ask her whereabouts. If she wanted to tell me, it would need to be her decision. I felt peace about letting her go this time. Her calls reassured me she was at least alive. Her conversations were at first short and abrupt, but with time, they gradually returned to lengthier and friendlier communication between us. I wanted her to know I still loved her, but I had my protective guard up.

One night, she contacted my brother and sister-in-law, Angela's Uncle Harvey and Aunt Anne, and asked if she could visit with them. She was lonely and wanted to be with family, she said. At her request, Harvey met her on a street corner. When Harvey arrived, he saw a patrol car parked next to the curb. Angela stood there arguing with the police officer. Not knowing what to expect, Harvey hesitantly got out of his car, and explained to the officer that he was Angela's uncle. The police officer let her leave with him. Angela didn't try to explain what it was about, and Harvey didn't ask. That evening, at their home, she saw her favorite great-grandmother, Grandma Hunt, who was also visiting Harvey and Anne. Their visit was awkward. Grandma Hunt could only express her love and concern for Angela. No one really talked about Angela's life. They knew she would be unwilling to discuss it, and their time together would be cut short if they initiated any confrontation. A couple of hours after dinner, Angela told Harvey she needed to leave. The heaviness and sadness that hung with Angela's presence left each of them with sorrow. Harvey expressed his feelings of helplessness as he dropped her off at that same street corner, and watched her disappear into the night.

It wasn't long after that when she called me.

"Would you and Dad like to visit me?"

She caught me off guard.

"You have to promise me that you won't call the police if I tell you where I am."

"Angela, I've already given you my word. Call me back. I'll talk to your dad."

Farewell, My Free Bird

Keith and I hesitated to visit her, knowing she was set up at this motel for prostitution. We didn't want to give the appearance of our approval. Yet, she still needed to know we loved her. If there was any way to win her back without rescuing her, we wanted to be open to it.

She was excited when she heard we were coming. We agreed to meet her just off a main highway at a convenience store. We didn't see her at first. Keith drove slowly through the parking lot, wondering if she had changed her mind. Just then, she rushed from inside the store toward our car. She hopped into the back seat, and started directing Keith to her motel. We drove about a mile through a crime-ridden part of town. The longer we drove the seedier it got.

"There it is! Turn left, Dad!"

This motel was dirty and even dingier than the last motel she had stayed in. The horseshoe-shaped building was clearly neglected. The manager stood outside his door watching us suspiciously. With his uncombed hair, disheveled appearance, and blood-shot eyes, he looked as if he were recovering from a hangover. We entered her tiny room. Covers were thrown on her bed. For lack of any other place to put them, clothes were scattered on a threadbare chair and on top of the tottering dresser. A small kitchenette adjoined the bedroom.

"Excuse the mess. I cleaned up a little this morning." She stood smiling at us. "Well, what do you think of my place?"

I looked at Keith. What were we supposed to say? That it was a cheap dump, and we could hardly wait to leave because it hurt too much to see her living like this?

Avoiding her question, I walked toward the tiny kitchenette. "What's in here?"

She seemed delighted to show us her tiny stove and refrigerator. She opened the refrigerator door displaying the two artichokes she had purchased. A few drinks were the only other contents inside.

"I've learned to cook artichokes. I love to dip them in butter."

She closed the door.

"While you're here, could you drive me to the grocery store? I'm low on groceries. Wherever I go, I have to walk so it's hard for me to go shopping."

Doing anything to get out of this place sounded good. Keith waited in the car while we went into the grocery store. It amused me to watch her shop. She carefully compared prices and chose fresh fruit and vegetables, whole grain bread, and items that in the past she objected to eating when she lived at home. I stood in line next to her while she paid the bill. We helped carry the bags of food into the motel.

"What do you eat when you can't get to the store?" I asked.

"Sometimes I can get someone to take me to the grocery store. If I can't find someone to take me, I have a friend who will leave food outside my door. Usually, it's a bag with a hamburger and french-fries inside. There are a few people who watch out for me."

We stayed only a few minutes more. I felt sad leaving her and more confused than ever. Why was she choosing such a dangerous and lonely lifestyle? Why would she choose to live in this dump, sometimes without food, and at the mercy of strangers instead of at home?

I saw a police car turn into the motel and circle the building. I prayed quietly . . . *Lord, I don't know what's best for her but You do. If she would be safer in jail than here, please open the eyes of some policeman and have her arrested!*

A month later, Angela frantically called. "Mom, I need help! I have a serious infection. I need medication. I'm broke. Will

Farewell, My Free Bird

you meet me at the doctor's office and pay for the medicine? I'll pay you back later."

She suffered continually from the pain of infectious gonorrhea and syphilis. The last doctor we took her to warned her that she would never heal if she continued to be sexually active.

My first reaction was to help, but I promptly stopped myself. It would only serve as a bandage. And God had told me not to enable her anymore. But how could I say no to needed medication? I stalled for time, telling her to call me again in an hour. I reached Keith at work, asking him for advice. He struggled just as I did.

"Pray about it, and call me before the hour is up." I said.

I called Shawn, our pastor.

"Shawn, help! We told Angela we wouldn't help her in any way as long as she chose to live as she is. But should we say no to this?"

"I need time to think and pray about it. I'll call you back."

I knelt next to the bed. *Lord let us know what we should do. We need your wisdom right now!*

I felt God was telling me to go back to the verses He gave me for Angela in Psalm 107. I found my Bible and opened to Psalm 107. As I read the verses He had given me two years before in this Psalm, verses twelve and thirteen stood out, as if God alone were speaking to me, giving me the answer I sought just minutes before. "*. . . they stumbled and there was no one to help.* **Then** *they cried out to the Lord in their trouble, and He saved them from their distress.*" I knew what I was to do! I was to leave her in God's hands. He had made it clear to me. I was not to help. He wanted her to cry out to Him.

The phone rang.

Keith said, "I know this is hard, but I don't think we should give her the money for the medication."

Shawn called. "I almost told you to buy the medication for her, but since I've prayed about it, I feel strongly that you're not supposed to help her this time."

It was yet another confirmation to me that God was in this decision.

Then Angela called.

"Mom, are you going to help me get the medication?"

"No Angela, we're not going to buy it for you."

"What do you mean? You don't understand. I have to have it. I'm in pain. I have a serious infection. I have to have it today."

"I'm sorry. We can't help you this time." I cringed. This was so unnatural.

"I can't believe you're not going to help me. I guess you don't care."

"I know you don't understand this Angela, but . . . ."

"Sure, that's real love, Mom. All I'm asking for is medication. So, what am I supposed to do?"

"I don't know." I answered.

"Thanks a lot!" she yelled before hanging up on me.

I knew I did the right thing, yet I felt like I had been in a battle. I wasn't sure if I had won or lost. I stood up to walk away from the phone. Suddenly, I felt an unexpected and overwhelming peace consume me. I had never felt anything like this before. A refreshing confidence and quiet strength replaced my anxiety. I became filled with more joy than I thought I could contain.

It was two weeks before I heard from Angela again. She called, her speech was rapid, and I could barely understand her.

"Mom, you've got to give me my social security number!"

I read it to her over the phone, trying to contain my curiosity. She was never concerned about her social security number before.

Excited and unashamed, she unfolded her dramatic experience.

"You're not going to believe this. I was going to buy some stolen property from this guy I met. He said he'd feel safer if we went to his car to finish the transaction. When we got into his car, he held me down and aimed a loaded gun at my head! He had this crazy expression on his face. He started to squeeze the trigger. I said a silent prayer to God telling Him that if He'd get me out of this I'd go straight, and I'd never do this again. I'd get a real job. Mom, God saved me! I know he did!"

She could hardly get the words out.

"All of a sudden, after I prayed, the guy looked puzzled. He just stared at me. He seemed confused. He took the gun away from my head, and said to me, 'I don't know what's happening. I was going to kill you.' Then, he screamed at me, 'You'd better get out of here, fast!' I jumped out of his car as quick as I could and ran to the phone booth to call you."

There was no doubt in her mind or mine that God had intervened. She repeated her social security number to me twice making sure she had it written down right before she hung up.

I was ecstatic; I wanted to scream my delight. I thanked God for His grace and miraculous intervention in saving my daughter's life. Maybe now Angela would choose to trust God and be free from this life that was destroying her.

Sadly, within days, Angela forgot her promise to God and returned to prostitution. I watched her fall even deeper into that damnable life.

I just want to be free from me, from life.

I just want peace.
I want to give you a chance at me . . .
But you don't understand the kind of life I lead.
Why can't life just stop me.
I'm in my own world,
And I won't let you get in because I am still in the end.
                              Angela, FREE BIRD

Chapter Thirteen

I AM THE LONELY IN YOUR HEART

"Turn to me and be gracious to me, for I am lonely and afflicted. The troubles of my heart have multiplied; free me from my anguish." (Psalm 25:16-17)

Once Angela was eighteen, she began working at different massage parlors. She started showing up at the house and leaving in taxicabs.

One day, a police officer from a nearby city called, "Your daughter is in our custody. We've arrested several people from a massage parlor. She was inside the building and can be booked for suspicion of prostitution. She told us her father is a policeman."

"That's correct." I answered.

"If this was by chance a mistake, or her first arrest, we can release her until she needs to appear in court."

I could see he was trying any way he could to legally help a fellow police officer.

"This wasn't a mistake." I told him. "Angela's been involved in prostitution for a long time, and it would be best for her if she was arrested." It hurt to say that and I felt disloyal. But, it would be wrong to jump in and save her from the consequences. I remembered the night I asked God to open some policeman's eyes, for her to be arrested if He knew it could help her and keep her safe.

"Hey, it's dangerous for her to be involved in these massage parlors. First thing you know, they'll be sending her all over the country. They never keep any of their girls in one place for very long. It's their way of avoiding being too well known by the police. Well, if there's anything I can do; listen, tell your husband to call me when he gets in."

Keith returned his call, and before the conversation ended, the police officer had decided to release Angela until her court date.

Angela bought a new dress and appeared in court, only to have it continued to another date. The next court date, she didn't show up at all. A warrant was made for her arrest.

It was the beginning of her being sent from place to place by the people she worked with in the massage parlors. She went to Nevada, then San Diego, and other parts of California.

On my birthday in November, Angela showed up unexpectedly in a taxicab.

"Mom, I want to buy you a dress for your birthday. Could we go to the mall? It would be fun to spend time together."

Knowing the source of her money, I was not enthused about going shopping, but I said yes because it seemed so important to her that we spend time together. And it was important to me also.

We went to the mall, and she picked out the dresses she wanted me to try on. Finally, we found the dress she approved of. It did look nice. The bright blue color complemented my skin tone, and the style was flattering.

"That's it, Mom. Do you like it?"

"I love it."

I knew I had made the right decision when I accepted her gift and saw her excitement. She found herself a dress, and proudly took them to the cash register. I winced when I saw her pull out her wallet that was loaded with money. I felt extremely awkward, but I gave her a hug and thanked her.

As soon as we got home, she insisted we try on our dresses and show off for Keith. She was pleased as we paraded in front of her dad.

"Wow. You both look great!"

"Do you like Mom's dress? Doesn't she look pretty?"

Six weeks passed before she came home again. It was a few weeks before Christmas. I was upstairs when I heard the front door open. I was surprised to hear Angela's voice.

"Mom? Where are you? I need you down here."

When I came downstairs, I saw tears streaming down her face.

"Did the hospital call you?"

"No. What happened?"

I led the way to the living room, and we sat on the sofa.

"Mom, I just left the emergency room. I over-dosed on cocaine. I called the paramedics from my motel, but then I got scared and hung up. But they had traced my call and sent an ambulance to the motel. The paramedic told me if they would have arrived just a few minutes later, I would've been dead."

By this time we were both teary. She laid her head on my lap. I stroked her hair as she continued. She spoke slowly, hesitating after each sentence.

"My way is not working. I'm finding out that my friends are not my friends. I can see now that my life is going nowhere."

I wanted to advise her, but I knew better. This would have to be her choice.

"So what are you going to do, Angela?"

"I don't know what I can do. What kind of job could I get?"

Her choices were limited because of her rebellion and life style that had kept her out of school since the tenth grade. I had never seen her so down. I knew that Angela would have to hit bottom before she would ever see her need for help.

"Angela, if I knew you were serious, I'd do anything to help you."

We discussed different options, and I was more hopeful than ever before. She stayed with us and regained her strength.

During that time she even had a real date. She came to me a few hours before the young man was to pick her up at the house.

"When I go out with him, am I supposed to pay for the dinner or is he?"

"Well, if he asked you out then he probably intends to pay for it. Let him treat you and enjoy it."

"Gosh, I guess I don't know very much about these things."

She returned home, pleased with how the evening went.

"Thanks for the advice. It worked out great!"

Also, during that time we had some interesting conversations. I had read a book, "The Blessing." It explained how to give a blessing to those you love by words and actions. It was easy to do this for Keith and the boys. But, it was difficult knowing how to give Angela a blessing. I could tell her I loved her, but I couldn't tell her how proud I was of the choices she was making for her life. I could say how special she was to me, but I couldn't say how much joy she gave me. I prayed God would show me a way to bless Angela in a way that would be meaningful to her.

Farewell, My Free Bird

One evening, she and I were talking and I said to her, "Angela, someday I would like for you and me to write a book."

"What do you mean?" she asked.

"I would like for you to be able to share the struggles that you're going through now, and I would share what I'm going through as a parent. I know you're going to make it, because God has given me promises for you. And then we could share together what God has done in and through your life."

She pondered what I had just told her.

Then she said, "I want to see the promises God gave you for me."

We opened the Bible together. She sat, listening intently while I read the Scriptures from the books of Psalm and Isaiah.

"You know," she said, "there have been many times I've been alone and in trouble, and I asked God to help me, and He did."

"Angela, God does hear you when you ask Him for help. He is working in your life, and He loves you. Let Him be in control. You can trust Him. He cares for you, and He wants the best for you. Someday, you're going to make it. You're going to be free from these addictions. You've shared with me that it's your desire to help others, and I know God will use what you're going through to help other people so they can be free too."

Her face softened, and the anxiety left. This had been important for her to hear. I realized later, when I crawled under the covers and contemplated the day's events, that God had given me a special way to impart to my daughter a meaningful blessing.

It was Christmas time again, and Angela was home. Soon, more family would arrive. Carl, our oldest son, was taking military leave to be home for Christmas, and my brother Tom and his family would be visiting from Canada. We had so much fun together that year. It was a wonderful and memorable Christmas day.

A few days after Christmas, Angela received news that her friend Marie had been killed in a car accident.

She told me, "Marie was driving home at two in the morning. Her brakes went out and her car rammed into a telephone pole. She's dead."

I had met Marie just a few weeks before, when Angela and she came to the house to show me a new outfit Angela had bought. Marie and she *'worked'* together. Angela started crying as she walked to her room, shutting the door behind her.

With each passing day, the cycle was returning. Angela became more difficult to get along with. I was afraid of losing her again. I tracked down a lady whom I had recently heard on the radio. Norma Ashby had been a prostitute at one time. Now, she was helping girls in the Los Angeles area who desperately wanted a way out of this addictive, bizarre lifestyle. Norma counseled me, encouraging me to enforce the bottom line rules we had established for Angela, one being she could live at home only if she was willing to stop the vicious cycle of drugs, alcohol, and prostitution. She wanted to talk to Angela. Angela agreed to talk with her on the phone.

Norma encouraged her to see her need for help and told her she wasn't likely to break her addictions on her own. Norma's profound insights impressed Angela. She understood Angela's inner conflict and the overwhelming mixed emotions she struggled with. Norma knew the addictions would call Angela back to the streets, and that she was struggling with whether to continue in prostitution or leave it. She knew that even though a great amount of money passed through Angela's hands, she would always be broke. Norma offered to help her by getting her into a home with other girls who were struggling as she was. Angela refused.

"I don't want to be confined again."

I appealed to her. "Please, Angela. It's only for a short time. What is a few months out of your life, if it meant you could be free for the rest of your life?"

"I'm not going to any home with restrictions. I've had enough of that in the hospital and in juvenile hall!"

Several days later, she dressed up to go to work at a restaurant, or so she said. She called a taxi, and when it arrived, she started out the door; then she called back to me, "Don't wait up for me. I'll probably be late."

I walked over to the living room window and watched as she climbed into the back seat of the cab. The taxi drove up the street and out of sight. I knew she wouldn't be coming back.

I saw you sitting there on the chair.
Your mind wondering dreams you've always wanted to share,
But so afraid because they are dreams only you believe.
I know you're awake at night wanting to cry of your emptiness,
The need of someone to be there,
But it's too late.
I know my friend because you are me.
I am the lonely in your heart,
I am the deep down hurt who feels ripped apart,
I am alone when all is near,
I am always in fear.
I am PAIN.

Angela, FREE BIRD

Angela holding Lisa's newborn, Melissa, on Christmas 1985

*Angela's 16th Birthday Party in the Hospital
Angela standing with Grandpa and Grandpa Byrne, Great
Grandma Hunt sitting*

"Ready for School" Angela and Carl

Angela in her room at the court-ordered placement in Hollywood, CA., 1985

"Best Friends" Paula and Angela

L to R Aunt Mary, Lisa, Kevin, David, Uncle Joe

L to R Carol, Keith, Jason, Travis, Angela, Carl
Christmas 1983

Funeral services at Hillside Chapel at Rose Hills Mortuary in Whittier, CA., 1987

Los Angeles motor officers line up to make a path for family members carrying Angela in her casket to her final resting place, while the piper plays, "Going Home."

"Saying Goodbye" Family and friends at Angela's gravesite

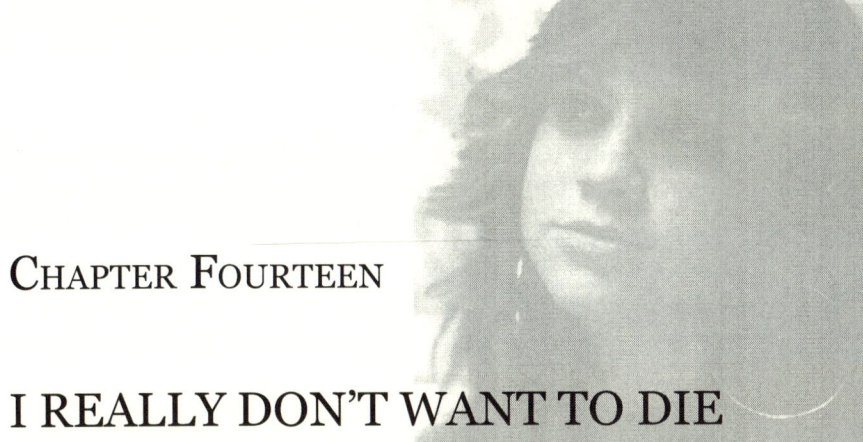

Chapter Fourteen

I REALLY DON'T WANT TO DIE

"Show me, O LORD, my life's end and the number of my days; let me know how fleeting is my life." (Psalm 39:4)

We knew we could no longer give Angela free reign to come and go as she pleased. More than once she had come home burnt out from the world, only to regain her strength and then return again to those things and those people who were destroying her. Believing we were helping her and remembering Norma Ashby's advice, we wrote Angela a letter.

> Angela,
> We love you. You are welcome to come home to visit, but until you make a firm decision to leave prostitution and get help for your addictions, you can't spend the night here or live at home. Remember we are here to help you if you are willing to get help. Also, Norma Ashby is available and willing to help you.
>
> Dad and Mom

We included Norma's phone number.

She was upset with us when she read the letter. Eventually, though, she accepted our rules. Occasionally, she stopped by the house to visit us, but always in a taxi. One morning, Angela sat on my bed talking to me while I fixed my hair.

Through the mirror I saw her glance at her watch.

"Mom, will you drive me to work?"

I turned toward her, surprised she would even ask.

"Of course not!"

"Why not?"

"Angela, think about it. You want me, your mom, to drive you to a place where you'll be prostituting yourself? No way. I can't do that."

I watched her seriously contemplate what I had said.

"Yeah, I guess you're right."

Angela had become street-wise, but her naiveté often puzzled me.

Weeks later, she moved from one massage parlor to another. This time she lived in the city of Palmdale. Each phone call I received, she told me of her plans to leave prostitution and attend cosmetology school.

"In another month I'll have enough money saved. Then, I'll come home and go to school." It sounded good, except her plans were always for *some day.*

Angela tried her best to convince me that her life was wonderful and exciting. One evening, while talking on the phone with her, I sensed she was unusually sad. The typical enthusiasm, or sometimes forced enthusiasm, was missing from her voice.

She told me, "I'm afraid of getting AIDS. I'm bleeding in between my periods. I guess I should go to the doctor. I am going to get out of this life soon. Maybe by the end of next month . . ."

I interrupted, "Angela, stop talking about getting out of it. Just do it!"

"I will. I just need to save a little more money. It won't take long. Then, I'll be home. You'll see."

I continued to pray for my daughter. Often when I prayed for Angela, the circumstances worsened. I had learned not to be discouraged by what I observed. I knew there was a spiritual battle going on and that Satan would not let go of his hold on her easily. But he couldn't steal the victory God had promised, and I sensed that victory was near. Evidence of this warfare proved to me that my prayers, and those of so many others, were effective and in the process of being answered. No, instead of being discouraged, I would get excited.

It was in February when I felt an extreme heaviness permeate my every thought and action. I felt an overwhelming need to pray and fast for Angela. I had prayed and fasted for her in the past, but this was different. This came with such intense urgency. I sensed a serious battle was being fought for Angela in the spiritual realm.

I spent periods of time praying and fasting. Several of my friends came alongside, and together we asked God to fulfill the promises He had given me for Angela. We fervently prayed that she be set free from the strongholds of addictions that bound her and kept her captive. We asked that she would see her value and worth and be set free from the lies and deceptions that she believed about herself, *and* that she would make the right choices necessary to be set free. We felt a peace and excitement knowing God was in this and knowing He was working.

One Sunday night, our church group met as usual at our pastor's home for our Sunday night service. At the close of the meeting, our pastor, Shawn, asked for prayer requests. I told them of the unusual urgency I had felt the past few weeks for Angela. Shawn read from the Scriptures in Psalm 107, the promises God had given me for Angela, almost three years before. Then, we bowed our heads and earnestly interceded for her. When we finished, I felt relieved, confident of God's inevitable intervention.

Suddenly, a man sitting across the room looked up and his face broke into a smile.

He spoke, "When we were praying I had a picture of Angela. I saw her tied up with heavy cords. As we prayed, I saw the cords unravel, and she was being set free."

Su said, "I had a picture of her, too. She was stuck in a deep pit. We were digging her out and calling to her . . . We're almost there Angela! We're almost there!"

I felt encouraged. God was working. She would be free. When Keith and I returned home, Angela and Travis were chatting on the phone.

"Mom, Angela's on the phone. She wants to talk to you."

She started telling me how wonderful her life was.

I stopped her. "Angela, God has put you so heavily on my mind. Something is going on. What is it?"

For a few seconds, she remained silent. Then, her voice changed.

"Mom, it's awful!" For the next several minutes she poured out her frustrations and her fears. "I'm having such a hard time. Everything's going wrong. I'm still bleeding heavy in-between my periods. I don't want to do this anymore. But, they don't understand. I have a lump in my breast. I have an appointment to see the doctor at the end of April. I hope it's not cancer. I guess my way isn't working." Before saying goodbye, she said, "Mom, please keep praying for me. It won't be long before I come home."

Farewell, My Free Bird

A few days later, she called just to ask if I was still praying for her.

I reassured her of my prayers and of my love.

"Thanks," she said. "I have to go now. Bye."

It looked promising. I hoped the time would come soon that she would freely choose to get help and be released from the deadly chains that gripped her.

After that conversation, every time she called, it seemed important to her to know she was being covered in prayer.

Her next move was to Oakland, California. This time, she lived in an apartment with two other women. April was fast approaching, and Angela talked of her plans to come home for her nineteenth birthday. This created an awkward situation for Keith and me. She was still actively involved in prostitution and was planning to take a trip to Las Vegas before she came home. We reminded her of our letter and told her she needed to make other arrangements for spending the night.

"But, I'm coming home for my birthday!"

We wished we didn't have to say no to her, but we stood our ground.

"We know it's your birthday, Angela. But you'll have to make other arrangements for the night."

"Don't worry," she said. "If I come, I'll find another place to stay." She was hurt. It would be so natural to welcome her with open arms under different circumstances. We hoped someday, she'd understand.

The week of her birthday, she called to verify the date and time of her arrival.

"Do you still have another place to spend the night?" I asked.

"Yes, my friend is expecting me."

Birthdays were always a special time in our family, a time to celebrate. I invited Paula for dinner, and on April 8th prepared one of Angela's favorite meals. I decorated the kitchen and bought her favorite strawberry-filled cake with her name written on top. Everything was ready and in place. I hoped this would be a special night for her.

By six in the evening, Paula called, wondering if Angela had arrived yet. By this time, none of us were sure if or when Angela would be coming home. Instead of waiting, Paula decided to eat at her home.

By seven, we had eaten. Travis and Jason left the house to attend a game at the high school. At eight-thirty, I started taking the decorations down in the kitchen when we heard a loud bang on the front door. Keith opened the door. Angela stood on the porch with her arms full of suitcases. The taxi pulled away from the curb.

"Will you help me carry in my suitcases?"

Keith took her suitcases from her and set them on the living room floor. Keith and I looked at each other. We hoped this didn't mean another unpleasant confrontation.

"I'm sorry I'm late. I spent last night in Las Vegas. My plane left later than it should have."

She leaned over and opened one of her suitcases. "Let me show you the new outfit I bought in Las Vegas." She pulled out a light blue dress decorated in western trim, with silver conchos.

"Isn't it pretty? See, it matches my boots." She raised her foot to show me the ankle high white, western high-heeled boots she wore.

As we visited with her, we noticed she was extremely edgy. She spoke rapidly, racing from subject to subject. It had been two months since we had seen her. I studied her pale, gaunt face and noticed she was thinner than the last time we saw her. This life was taking its toll.

I gave her my present, a silver necklace. "That's pretty," she said holding it up. "Thanks." She placed the necklace back into the box.

"I think I'll call Paula."

After she hung up the phone, I asked her, "Where are you spending the night?"

Her nervous smile conveyed to us she had no plans. "Well, umm, I had it all set up, but my friend had to leave town. So, I'm hoping you'll let me stay here."

Keith and I suspected this might happen. We were prepared.

Keith said, "We told you before you came that you couldn't stay here."

"It's not my fault it didn't work out. I don't have any other place to go."

Keith spoke, "We'll get a night at the motel for you."

I said, "In the morning, I'll pick you up. We can go shopping and enjoy the day together."

"I spent my own money to fly home and be here for my birthday. I can't believe you won't let me stay just one night in my own home."

Keith answered, "It was understood before you came, Angela. This is no surprise."

"Well, I'm going to leave then. I can't waste my time here. I've got important things I need to do."

A knock on the door interrupted our conversation. Angela let Paula in. Her strained greeting alerted Paula that something was wrong.

"Paula, would you drive me to the airport?"

Paula looked confused. "I guess I can take you." Paula glanced at us.

"They won't let me stay here, so I have to call the L.A. airport and get a flight out of here tonight."

"If you have to leave tonight, I'll take you." Keith said.

"I'd rather Paula took me." She looked over at Paula. "You don't mind, do you?" "Well, maybe I could ask Ron to go with us. He knows the way better than I do, and then I wouldn't be driving home by myself."

In a flurry, Angela started making phone calls. She called several different airports before she found an available flight. The plane would leave at midnight. She made several calls to her friends in Oakland to arrange to be picked up.

She left with Paula without even saying goodbye to us. I was trembling. I felt like a train had run over me. I walked upstairs and fell on my bed, feeling broken and angry.

The next morning, Paula's mother, Mary, called me. Mary was not only my neighbor, but a close friend.

"Angela missed her flight last night," she said. "Paula drove her back, and Angela checked into the motel just a few blocks from us. Paula got home really late. She barely got out of bed this morning to go to work. Paula said when Angela missed her flight, she kept calling you from the airport but no one answered."

Fortunately, the phone in our room had been unplugged.

"When Angela couldn't get through, she became angry and started cursing you. Paula told me before she left this morning that Angela's not much of a friend, and she's not much of a daughter either. I've never seen Paula so upset with her."

The operator interrupted our conversation.

"I have an emergency call from Angela Noe. Will you accept?"

"No." I abruptly answered.

I had cried myself to sleep last night. I awoke this morning still hurting, but relieved Angela had returned to Oakland, so I thought. I was determined I wouldn't allow myself to go through another repetition of what had happened last night.

She had probably called to ask me to take her to the airport. I didn't want to see her or talk to her. She wouldn't take no for an answer. Trying to avoid being put in a position of being harassed or manipulated, I left the house early planning to be gone for most of the day. Hopefully, she would take a cab to the airport and be gone when I returned.

About two in the afternoon, I walked into the house and smelled the odor of cigarette smoke. I walked down the hall toward the den and heard her voice.

"Where have you been? I thought you said we could go shopping today?"

"Angela, how did you get in here?"

"No one was here, so I came through the window. I need you to drive me to the airport," she demanded.

"We offered to take you last night, and you refused. After the way you treated us, I'm not taking you anywhere. You can call a cab."

"What do you mean the way I treated you? You didn't let me stay here." She smiled. "You'll have to take me to the airport or I'm not leaving."

I walked upstairs. She followed me.

"Maybe you'll have to call the police to get me out of here."

I picked up my purse and keys to leave. If I stayed, I would say something I'd regret. She was successfully pushing me. I drove the car, not sure where I would go. I could hardly see the road through the tears. Keith would be home from work soon. He could handle her. I had no more strength to face her and to be hurt again.

I loved her, but I felt overwhelmed by anger and despair. It was painful to see her self-destruct. I knew my anger was in response to the pain I felt, and it was my protection from being hurt by her anymore. I wished I could hold her and tell her I loved her and that it would make a difference. But, I couldn't get through to her. She wouldn't let me in. The more I tried to help her, the worse it got. It seemed so unnecessary. Why couldn't we be free to love each other? *Why, Angela? Why are you resisting those who love you?* I felt as though I were fighting a force greater than both of us.

Keith met me at the door when I returned.

"Where have you been?" Before I answered, he continued, "You shouldn't have left her here in the house alone," he sternly reprimanded me. "You never know what she might do when she's like this. Jason and I are leaving to take her to the airport."

Keith left to get the car out of the garage. They loaded her suitcases into the trunk. I stood in the kitchen, watching Angela who stood in the hallway by the front door. For a few seconds our eyes met. I felt that both of us wanted to say something to the other. But, the hurt and anger we each felt dominated our emotions. She turned and walked out the door. Neither one of us said goodbye. I heard the car door shut and listened as they drove off.

We had weathered these storms before. It would take some time, but we would eventually be on talking terms again. Next time, though, I vowed to be more cautious.

Paula's mother, Mary, called me the next morning, "I feel guilty. Angela ran up to the house to say goodbye to me before Keith drove her to the airport. I bawled her out for the way she had treated everyone." This was unlike Mary, who usually showed only her concern for Angela. "Carol, I was just so mad at her. I couldn't help it. Now, I feel bad. She showed me the necklace you gave her for her birthday. She really likes it."

The following weekend, I left with my friends from church to attend a women's retreat in Desert Hot Springs. The speaker captivated us with her insights and instructive teachings.

Between workshops, the women relaxed by the pool. We finished the retreat with a communion service. As we took our turns going up to receive communion, the speaker laid her hands on us and prophesied over each one of us. It fascinated me. Unlike this lady, I knew these women and some of the problems they struggled with. She spoke words to them that only God could have revealed to her. The room contained the presence of God. I wrote the words of prophecy she gave to me in a notebook. They were words of hope for Angela that encouraged me and reminded me of the promises God had given me for her.

Carl came home on leave from Yuma, Arizona, for the Easter holiday. Angela called the Saturday before Easter to talk with him.

"Carl is gone for the afternoon." I said.

Our voices were strained toward each other, but not unkind.

"Would you have him call me when he gets home? I haven't seen him for a long time, and I want to talk to him."

"I'll tell him you called."

Angela admired Carl, especially since he had become a Marine. She often told him how proud she was of him. Carl returned her phone call, and politely spoke with her for a few minutes before saying goodbye.

So many others, friends and family members, let me know of similar frustrations with Angela. They spoke of the intense guilt they felt when they had encounters with her. Their efforts to reach her were returned by Angela's manipulation and stubborn determination to do *her own thing*. With the passage of time, she had left a trail of hurt and angry people who were no longer willing to help her. Contact with Angela made everyone painfully aware of their own helplessness.

Carl left a few days later, on his motorcycle, to return to the Yuma Marine Corps Air Station. I prayed for his safety as he drove down the street and out of sight.

On Sunday, April 26th, we awoke to the sun shining in our bedroom.

"Why don't we go out to lunch after church with Su and Shawn?" I asked.

Keith liked the idea. This was our pastor and his wife's anniversary week.

They graciously accepted our invitation, and that afternoon as we sat around the table, our conversation led to Angela. Shawn had become a pastor, counselor, and friend to Angela. They had established a close bond, and Angela often called Shawn just to touch base with him.

Shawn said, "The last time I talked with Angela, she asked me how she could tell some of her friends, who she thought had strange beliefs, about Jesus. I explained it to her the best I could. She said to me, 'Shawn, if only you were here, I know you could convince them about Jesus.'" Shawn expressed his own frustration at Angela's continual refusal to leave prostitution.

"It's a miracle she's alive." Shawn said.

Oh, how well Keith and I knew that.

That evening, we sat in Shawn and Su's living room for our Sunday night church service. Wayne, our worship leader, played his guitar. Together, we sang, "I Surrender All." I had heard it so many times before, but this time as I listened to the words I thought of Angela. I thought of the last time I saw her and how painful it was for her and me and the rest of the family. I thought of the promises God had given me for her. I thought of how she would call me and ask for prayer. It was like there were two Angelas: the sweet, wonderful, and caring Angela who had so much potential and wanted to *make it,* and the Angela who was driven by her rebellion and addictions.

Farewell, My Free Bird

"I surrender all. All to Thee my Blessed Savior, I surrender all."

I closed my eyes and lifted my hands. I completely surrendered my daughter to God. How could I have known that Angela had only a few hours left to live and that this very night she would be murdered?

For two days, I went about my normal activities. On Tuesday afternoon, the call came from the San Francisco Police Department telling us that our daughter was a homicide victim.

As I lay in bed that Tuesday night after the phone call, struggling with the unbearable pain of Angela's death, agonizing questions swirled in my head. How could Angela be dead? From Sunday night until Tuesday, how could I have not have known that Angela was dead?

And, God, what about the promises? I know that You gave them to me for Angela . . . You're not a God who lies. If anyone was wrong, I was; but I'm sure You gave them to me. God, is she with You?

I remembered Angela as a little girl kneeling beside me, telling God that she wanted to be His child and sincerely asking Jesus to forgive her sins and to come into her heart. I knew that salvation meant not only accepting Jesus as Savior, but also accepting Him as Lord, and giving Him control of our lives. As a young girl growing up, I saw her desire to serve God. She loved to learn about Jesus. She prayed earnestly for relatives and friends, while sometimes crying at night for those who didn't know Him. But, with her life the way it was these last few years, I had a nagging doubt. *God, I must know. Is she with You? I don't want others trying to comfort me by saying . . . Oh, she's with the Lord. I have to know from You. Please God, I have to know!*

Sometimes I think that I'm not really present at my life,
As though it goes without my permission.
Sometimes although I don't want to die,
I want to stop living.
I want to climb into the other side of my face,
And observe my expressions without having them.
Sometimes, and only once in a while, I want to stop living,
But I really don't want to die.
                              Angela, FREE BIRD

Chapter Fifteen

THE DAY IS NEW

> *"My soul finds rest in God alone; my salvation comes from Him. He alone is my rock and my salvation; He is my fortress, I will never be shaken." (Psalm 62:1-2)*

Our lives had been turned upside down. The trip to the mortuary the next morning seemed like a continuation of a bad dream. We wandered aimlessly in the dismal room examining cold and empty caskets. We had almost decided on one lined with pink satin, when I glanced to the back of the room and saw an opened casket that displayed a tapestry of praying hands laid against a luxurious ivory, silk background. I remembered Angela's phone calls.

"Mom, will you pray for me?"

The last few months of her life, being prayed for had become very important to Angela. Keith and I agreed that this casket with the praying hands would be the one. A funeral attendant drove us to see the gravesites. He showed us a plot in a peaceful location with an ivy covered fence nearby. On the other side of the fence was a street, but we could barely hear the sound of traffic. I remembered times when life seemed overwhelming and frustrating for Angela. She would say, "I need to get away for a while to be by myself." But, she never liked to be away from people for very long. This would be perfect for her.

"We'll take this one," Keith said.

He cried as we drove off, squeezing my hand.

"I hope she likes it," he said.

When we returned home, Carl and Jason sat at the kitchen table eating breakfast, their faces weary from lack of sleep. Travis had gone to school. I noticed the dishes had been done, and the house was picked up.

"Su, Carrie, and Debbie came over this morning and cleaned the house," Carl said. "They left a casserole in the refrigerator."

Appreciation and relief overwhelmed me. It was just the beginning of many expressions of love that our family and friends would show us in the days to come.

Keith's parents and sister were flying into the L.A. airport later that evening. My brother, Tom, from Canada was also on his way. People came and went throughout the day. Frank and Betty, our neighbors and close friends, had lost a son three years earlier. They understood our pain. I told Betty of my fears about seeing Angela.

"She was so brutally stabbed and shot. I'm afraid of seeing terror on her face. I may see more revealing details of what happened those last horror-filled moments of Angela's life. I don't know if I can handle that."

Betty gently encouraged me to see her. "It's important for you to see her, Carol. You need to say goodbye to her."

She was right. I knew I had to see her. Ever since we were told of Angela's murder, I couldn't let go of the thought that, just maybe, this still might be a bizarre mistake. Maybe this girl wasn't Angela. Then, I would remind myself of her *'Free Bird'* tattoo, the fingerprints, and of her friends who saw her leave the apartment and never return. I needed to settle the unrest in my mind. Regardless of my fears, I had to see for myself that it was Angela. I needed to say goodbye to her.

That evening, Travis came to me and said, "Mom, the last day Angela was home, she told me that she received a phone call from one of her friends in Oakland warning her not to return, because she might be in danger. Angela said she was going anyway. I tried to convince her not to go and told her she was being stupid if she returned. She just shrugged her shoulders and said to me, 'You know I can't stay here. Besides, even if I get hurt a little, nothing bad is going to happen to me.'"

Oh Lord! Why didn't she heed the warning? Tormenting thoughts consumed me. If only she had come and told us she was in danger. If only I had reassured her of my love the last time we were together. Did she know as she lay on the ground dying that I loved her? Did she know that our rules were meant to help her and not to reject her?

Paula's mother, Mary, came to visit and handed me a stained, worn paper. "Angela wrote this for me many years ago. I thought you might want to have it."

Angela had written . . . .

> To Mary,
> The day is new and the sky is blue.
> Don't delay. Do your work for today.
> The birds are singing, and the phone is ringing.
> The beach is near so have no fear.
> Have no fear, God is near.
> THE END, ANGELA

Angela's tender poem reminded me of the time when life was not so complicated for her.

Mary told me of a conversation Paula and Angela had the last night they were together. "Angela said to Paula, 'Let me know if there's a job opening where you work. I want to get a job and come home and live with my parents.'"

I stopped Mary. "She told Paula that?"

I felt overwhelmed with emotion and relief. Angela did know that we didn't reject *her*, but her lifestyle. She knew that we loved her. She knew she could come home if she chose to leave her destructive lifestyle.

Tomorrow, we would see Angela for the first time since she was murdered. She would be ready for viewing at 1:00 in the afternoon.

I went to bed that night dreading what would take place the next day. After several hours of struggling with my thoughts, I finally fell into a deep sleep. Before dawn, I suddenly awoke. I opened my eyes only to be consumed by darkness; I must have had a bad dream. Why did I feel so uneasy? As I became oriented, a cold chill washed over me. Oh no! Reality, harsh and cruel, reminded me of all the horrifying details. Angela! The phone call . . . she's gone! She's been murdered! Today, we would see her body. How I wished this could be a bad dream. The only sounds were the ticking of the clock and my muffled sobs as I ached for my daughter.

Later that morning, I went through the motions of getting ready. I felt edgy. I couldn't sit still or concentrate. My stomach turned and twisted with anxiety. Time moved ever so slowly until, finally, it was time to leave for the visitation.

Keith and I left the house. We exchanged anxious glances, dreading what had to take place. We had asked to be alone the first hour, before other family members would come. As we drove, my mind filled with thoughts of Angela.

My hope that someday Angela would turn from her destructive lifestyle and live a happy and productive life was

Farewell, My Free Bird

now shattered. My special dream that someday she and I would enjoy the intimate mother-daughter relationship we both desired was now destroyed. I thought of the promises God had given me for her. I didn't understand. I was confused. Yet, nothing could take away the assurance I still felt about God's promises for Angela.

I thought of how fun-loving and free my little girl could have been, if it hadn't been for the drugs, alcohol, and the destructive choices that sent her out on the streets and into prostitution.

It had been so painful to watch her self-destruct. I didn't know there could be a worse pain until now. I felt a sharp sting as we turned onto the mortuary grounds. We parked and got out of the car. My feet felt like clay as we walked toward the building. Jerry Powell, the police chaplain and our friend, met us inside. He knew of my fear about viewing Angela.

He warmly greeted us. "I saw your daughter, and I feel good about you seeing her." We followed him into the elevator. My stomach churned as we arrived on the second floor and the elevator door opened. We slowly walked down the long narrow hallway. I was trembling and clutched Keith's hand for support. Jerry stopped at a closed door. He stood back; this was the room. Keith and I paused and looked at each other. The color had drained from Keith's face. He turned the door handle cautiously and opened it.

We both gasped when we saw her raised head lying on the silk pillow in the casket. Keith called out, "Oh my God, Angela!" We hurried toward her. I cried out her name in disbelief. I automatically reached out to touch her hand. I quickly pulled back in shock. *Oh God, she's so cold!* I stroked her soft brown hair, being careful not to touch her cold face.

"She always liked it when I stroked her hair," I whispered softly.

How could it be that we were standing over our dead daughter?

"I love you, Angela." I spoke aloud.

Keith and I stood over the casket, with our eyes fixed on her. Suddenly, I saw what should have been obvious to us at first.

"Keith, look at her!"

Amazed, and in awe, we saw how radiant she was. She appeared the picture of health. She had never been so beautiful. Her face glowed with an unexplainable peace. There was a slight hint of a smile that spoke to us, *"It's alright, Mom and Dad."* I could almost hear her speak it. We felt God's grace. With our awareness, we experienced God's peace fill the room. This was truly a miracle. Somehow, I knew, this was the Angela of heaven. Restored! As I stood over her casket, I had a picture of the Lord tenderly holding my wounded daughter in His arms as she lay dying on the ground. I saw her totally oblivious to anything but His love and comfort. God revealed to me that He carried Angela in His arms from this life to eternal life and this is what we saw on her face.

Several minutes later, three women entered the room.

The oldest of the three spoke. "You must be Angela's parents?"

"Yes." I answered curious who these women were.

"We're Angela's friends." They walked toward her.

I realized these were women Angela had worked with in one of the massage parlors. How dare they come here! I stood frozen as they gathered near her casket. Tears fell from the young woman's face. The older woman touched Angela's hair. Everything inside of me wanted to reach out to stop her.

She spoke to Angela. "Angela, you always knew how to make me laugh. We loved you. I'm going to miss you."

She turned toward me. "We were shocked to hear of her death. I'm sorry."

They sincerely seemed to be grieving. I saw the pain in their eyes. I felt myself softening. I didn't understand this part of Angela's life, but these women had been her friends. I could see they loved her.

The younger woman spoke, her voice soft. "Angela told me she had a Great-Grandma Hunt."

"Yes, she did." I said.

"Her Grandma Hunt was her very favorite person. She loved her the most."

I nodded. Grandma had been on medication ever since she had heard of Angela's death. It would mean a lot to her to know this.

They only stayed a few minutes more. When they opened the door to leave, the younger woman stood in front of me as if wanting to reach out. She looked so sad, so pitiful. I put my arms around her and thanked them for coming.

Family and friends came throughout that day to see Angela and us. Many people were amazed how beautiful and radiant she looked.

Shawn told us, "When I first entered the room, I was met by an overwhelming peace that so permeated the room even before I saw Angela. The only other time I've ever felt it that strongly was a time when I witnessed to a dying man. He accepted Jesus Christ as his Lord and Savior on his death bed, and the room instantly filled with this same intensity of peace."

During the day Jason asked us, "Can I be alone with Angela?" We waited outside the room while he went in by himself. When he came out, he said he needed to talk to Shawn.

Later, he told me what had happened.

"When I stood over Angela, I asked, *'God, is my sister with you?'* God answered me right away . . . *'Yes, she's with me.'*"

I told Jason what God had revealed to me about Angela's last moments. God was very real to us. Our pain eased. We were strengthened by the miracles we were experiencing.

By evening, most of the family, including Carl, left to go home. Travis hadn't come. He handled his grief by working. We had ten minutes left before we needed to leave. I felt disappointed that he hadn't show up. However, five minutes before closing, he entered the room, looking scared and anxious. I had never seen him so tense. He stood in disbelief staring at Angela in her casket. I walked toward him, and placed my hand on his shoulder. I led him to the casket. He stood frozen, not taking his eyes off his sister.

Jason came alongside Travis, and stood with him.

Keith and I stepped outside in the hallway just as the attendant came to tell us it was time to go.

"Please, give us a few more minutes. My son just got here. He needs time to be with his sister."

The man glanced at his watch. "I'll be back in ten minutes."

A few minutes later, Travis came out of the room. He seemed as if it was all he could do to keep from running.

"I've got to go," he said.

He had driven his motorcycle.

Keith said, "Travis, go straight home. We'll see you there."

"I have to ride around for a while before I go home. I need to be alone."

He turned and hurried toward the elevator. Keith called out to him, "Please be careful, Travis! Oh God, I hope he doesn't do anything foolish," Keith said as Travis disappeared down the hallway.

Farewell, My Free Bird

Keith, Jason and I hurried into the room to spend the last few minutes with Angela. The three of us knelt down in front of her casket.

Keith spoke, "Thank you God for your grace in showing us that she's with You. Angela, we're all going to be together again someday. We love you and we're going to miss you."

We left the mortuary with a new hope. In the midst of our pain, we experienced a joy and peace that went beyond our understanding. The three of us drove home singing praises to God, aware that He had won the final victory in Angela's life. We knew without a doubt now that Angela was safely home with her precious Savior.

> *Who do I have? What can I say?*
> *Who can I trust every step of the way?*
> *I hope and I pray that there will be someone, someday,*
> *Someone to hold me, someone to care,*
> *Someone to be there to share all my fears.*
> *I'm always loving and caring and never receiving.*
> *When will someone love me for who I am?*
> *   Angela, FREE BIRD*

Chapter Sixteen

A GLIMPSE OF MY GOD

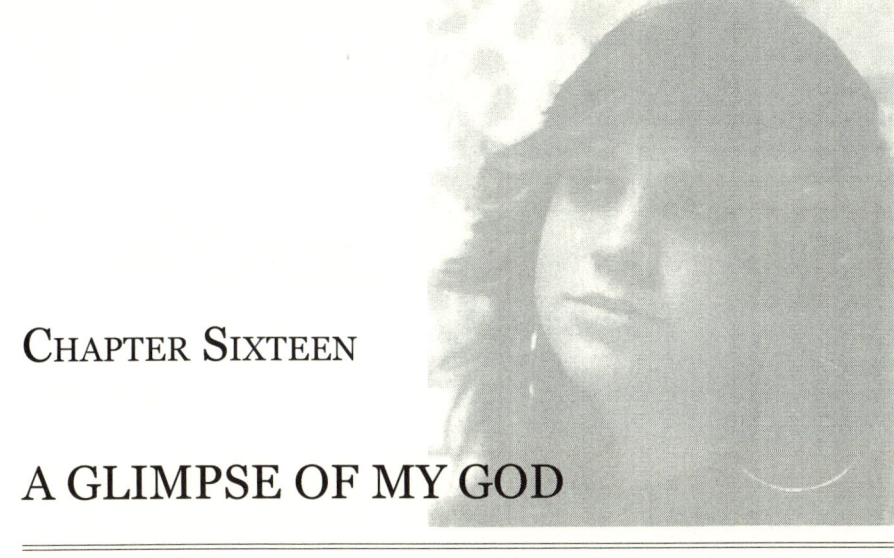

"Then they cried to the LORD in their trouble, and He saved them from their distress." (Psalm 107:19)

I awoke early the next morning. Keith's steady breathing let me know that he was in a deep sleep. Grabbing my pillow, I carefully got out of bed. I found my way in the dark to the small room that adjoins the bathroom. I picked up a notebook and pen and sat on the floor, propping the pillow against the wall to support myself. I remembered how peaceful and beautiful Angela looked yesterday in the viewing room and how God had comforted us with the message that He had rescued Angela in the last moments of her life.

I smiled as I recalled her radiant face. I imagined what it must have been like for her in His arms, oblivious to everything but His love. I felt thankful for God's victory and Angela's new freedom, but my heart was breaking. Now, I would have to live without her. I ached to hold her, to talk to her. There had been so many things left unsaid.

I began writing, pouring out my heart to Angela, expressing my deepest feelings of love. I told her all the things I would want her to hear. I could hardly see the pages through my tears. Soon daylight streamed in through the window, and I could hear the sound of birds singing. I remembered my *'Free Bird.'* She desired to be a free bird, but today she would be buried. Today we would say our goodbyes.

Keith awakened. "Carol, what are you doing?"

I handed him the letter. "I wrote this for Angela."

He read it and he put the papers down. His body shook as he began to sob. We held each other as we cried. Keith told me he felt this letter should be read at the funeral.

I had written this letter only for Angela, but because it was important to him I agreed.

Keith said, "At the funeral service I want to read the verses from the book of Psalm that God gave you for Angela three years ago." He reached for the Bible and opened it to Psalm 107:10-22. "Let me read them now to see if I'll be able to read them at the funeral without being too emotional."

I listened as he read and personalized those familiar verses, as I always did, when I read them and prayed them with her name in them.

> *"Angela sat in darkness and the deepest gloom, a prisoner suffering in iron chains, for she had rebelled against the words of God and despised the counsel of the most High. So He subjected her to bitter labor; she stumbled, and there was no one to help.* **Then,** *Angela cried out to the Lord in her trouble and He saved her from her distress. He brought her out of darkness and the deepest gloom and broke away her chains. Let her give thanks to the Lord for His unfailing love and His wonderful deeds for men, for He breaks down gates of bronze and cuts through bars of iron. Angela became a fool through her*

*rebellious ways and suffered affliction because of her iniquities. Angela loathed all food and drew near the gates of death. **Then**, she cried to the Lord in her trouble, and He saved her from her distress. He sent forth His word and healed her. He rescued her from the grave. Let her give thanks to the Lord for His unfailing love and His wonderful deeds for men. Let her sacrifice thank offerings and tell of His works with songs of joy."*

When Keith finished reading, I looked up at him in amazement.

"Keith, three years ago when God gave me those Scriptures, He told us that He was going to literally rescue Angela from the grave! And, in the viewing room he gave me the picture of Him being there for her when she was dying on the ground. He *did* rescue her from the grave. He actually carried her in His arms from this life, to eternal life!"

We sat quietly contemplating this. I had struggled intensely, wondering if we had been too harsh on Angela. Should we have helped her more than we did? Why did Angela and I have to be angry with each other the last time we were together? The pain of remembering her standing in the hallway, remembering that I didn't hug her or tell her that I loved her, haunted me. As I sat pondering these things, God's comforting, inaudible voice spoke to me, *"Carol, if you would have been there for her and done the things you're feeling guilty for now, she would have cried out to **you** in those last moments and not to **Me**"* I was starting to understand. Angela had come to a place where there was no one left to whom she could turn. Too many people had been hurt by her. God had allowed her to come to a place where it was only God and her. He had told me in these Scriptures that when there was no one else to help, then and only then, would she cry out to Him. I knew that Angela had cried out to God the night of her murder and God was there for her.

The house soon filled with family and friends. I felt like a robot, mechanically going through the motions of getting ready to leave for the funeral. I took the dress out of my closet that Angela had bought me for my birthday only five months before. I stopped to reflect on the fond memories this dress represented. I knew Angela would want me to wear it today.

Before we left for the funeral, family and friends gathered in the family room to pray. We joined hands. Keith and I prayed for God to be glorified this day. We prayed that other lives might be touched through our tragedy, and that Angela's death would not be wasted. Our friends prayed that God would give us strength. We held hands in a circle of love as Keith led out singing "Amazing Grace." I looked around in this emotion-filled room, silently expressing thankfulness for these precious friends and family members who had lovingly taken care of our meals, and spent long hours, each day, sitting by our side, comforting us.

Keith's parents drove with us to the cemetery. I watched people pass us in their cars, hurriedly going in different directions. How strange that life could go on as usual for others when ours had come to a screeching halt.

All too soon, we were on the mortuary grounds. I glanced at the large white stone building we had been in yesterday for the viewing. As we drove up the hill toward the chapel, roses in full bloom could be seen everywhere on the grounds. We were surrounded on both sides by lush, green rolling hills, marred only by the mass of grave markers. People stood over or sat next to graves. Some were crying; others appeared calm

Farewell, My Free Bird

as they visited their lost loved ones. This now would be a part of our lives.

We pulled into a parking space across from the large, stone chapel. The black hearse was parked at the back entrance.

Keith and I were surprised at the number of people who were present for Angela's funeral. There were friends we had expected to be here, but also many others we hadn't seen in years. Off to the side, uniformed motor officers were standing next to their motorcycles. We were overwhelmed by feelings of gratitude and of being loved. Words could not express how much their presence meant. We were greeted as we hurried toward the chapel. Just before we entered the building, I looked up to see birds flying everywhere over the chapel, singing loudly.

Angela's open casket had been set in the middle of the platform. A multitude of beautiful plants and flowers surrounded her open casket that displayed the praying hands against the soft silk background. Keith and I stood over her casket looking at her radiant and peaceful face, thanking God for His revelation to us that she was now with Him. We had just a few minutes to be with her before Keith took my hand and led me to our seats on the front row. The organ began to play.

Angela, if only you could be here to experience the love that is in this room for you.

Jerry, the police chaplain, read the poem we had chosen.

> "I'll lend you for a little time a child of mine for you to love while she lives, and mourn for when she is dead. It may be six or seven years or twenty-two or three; but will you 'til I call her back, take care of her for me? She'll bring her charms to gladden you, and should her stay be

brief, you'll have loving memories as solace to your grief. I cannot promise she will stay since all from earth return. But there are lessons taught down there I want this child to learn. I've looked the wide world over in my search for teachers true, and from all the throngs that crowd life's lanes I've selected you. Now, will you give her all your love, not think the labor vain, nor hate me when I come to call to take her back again? I fancied that I heard them say, 'Dear Lord, Thy will be done.' For all the joy thy child shall bring, the risk of grief we'll run. Shelter her with tenderness. Love her while you may. And for the happiness you've known, forever grateful stay; but, should the angels call for her sooner than you've planned, brave the bitter grief that comes and try to understand."

Then Jerry read the letter I wrote to Angela. I heard sounds of weeping as I wiped my own tears and held Keith's hand.

Shawn, our pastor, spoke next. He was struggling with his own feelings of grief as he talked tenderly about Angela. He also shared the gospel message from the pulpit.

When it was time, Keith went to the platform. Without losing his composure, he read the verses God had given us for Angela from Psalm 107 that now had new meaning for us. When he finished, he sat down next to me.

Wayne, our worship leader from church, sang Angela's favorite song, "Jesus Loves Me." I remembered Angela, four years old, banging on the piano keys with her doll sitting next to her. With gusto she sang out, *"Jesus loves me this I know, 'cause the Bible tells me so!"* I glanced at a heart-shaped flower arrangement sitting on the platform. On it was written, "Jesus Loves Me."

When Wayne finished singing, a kilted piper stepped out onto the platform from behind the curtain and began piping "Amazing Grace." Tears flowed freely throughout the chapel as the music touched many hurting hearts. The piper finished and stepped back behind the curtain. For a moment, a peaceful stillness filled the air and the only sounds were the birds singing outside and people softly crying.

The usher dismissed people row by row. Lines of familiar faces comforted us. Soon the church was empty, except for our immediate family. We went up to say our goodbyes to Angela. Jerry put the letter I had written next to Angela. I picked it up and gently placed it under her arms near her folded hands. I bent over and kissed her forehead before I turned and walked away.

We positioned our car in line behind the hearse. Other cars lined up behind ours. The Los Angeles Police Motor Officers were in front of the hearse, positioned two by two with their lights on and ready to lead the procession to the gravesite. I was deeply touched when Keith told me this honor was always reserved for fellow officers. This was the first time motor officers had done this for a policeman's child.

As we drove around the big circle drive we neared the gravesite. I turned and watched the long line of cars behind us. We pulled up to the curb. I saw the green cloth carefully placed over the mound of dirt.

Carl, Travis, and Jason, along with my brother Harvey, and brother-in-law, Joe, and David, Angela's favorite cousin, carried the casket from the hearse. The motor officers had formed two rows, facing each other, making a path for them. The piper stood in front of the line and led them through the line and to the gravesite as he piped the song, "Going Home."

I watched my sons and family, who dearly loved her, carry the casket to the platform. Shawn spoke, read Scriptures, and then announced that a reception would follow at our home.

I told one of the funeral attendants that I wanted a lock of Angela's hair. He took me to the casket and handed me a small knife with scissors attached. He opened the casket and helped me to step on the mound of dirt. Carefully, I leaned over and cut a lock of Angela's hair. I stroked her hair and took one long, last look.

"Goodbye, Sweetheart. I love you."

> *The wind brushing through my hair,*
> *The smell of the cold air is blowing my mind.*
> *The exotic feel of my thoughts,*
> *I will share with you for only a while.*
> *Then they are mine forever.*
> *Let me run naked through the air for a second,*
> *And catch a glimpse of my God.*
> *I know You are there.*
> *The wind and the air show me You are there.*
>
> *Angela, FREE BIRD*

Chapter Seventeen

RISE UP AND SPREAD YOUR WINGS

"He sent forth His Word and healed them; He rescued them from the grave." (Psalm 107:20)

I felt such intense pain that Angela was gone, yet I felt such intense joy that God had revealed to us that she was with Him. But now I wondered how we could live without her. Carl, Travis and Jason were deeply grieving for their sister, each handling their grief in their own way. I remember praying for each of them the day after the funeral. As I read my Bible in Isaiah 54, Verse 13, I felt that God was speaking to me through these verses . . .

"All your sons will be taught by the Lord, and great will be your children's peace."

I thanked Him for what I believed were promises for my sons. As I continued to read, God continued to speak through His Word . . . *"In righteousness you will be established: Tyranny will be far from you; You will have nothing to fear. Terror will be far removed; it will not come near you . . ."*

I stopped. *But God, how can this be? We just buried Angela yesterday.* He answered in the next verses . . . *"If anyone does attack you, it will not be my doing; whoever attacks you will surrender to you."*

I knew this had not been God's will for Angela, or His doing. But what does it mean whoever attacks you will surrender to you? Will there be contact with this man someday? I wondered about a trial. According to the detective the chances of that were very slim.

The police were unable to arrest the man they knew murdered Angela for lack of evidence. The potential witnesses were afraid of him and unwilling to cooperate. It would be a miracle if a murder trial would ever take place. Not completely understanding what these verses meant, I dated them, May 3, 1987.

I thought often about this faceless, nameless man who murdered Angela. God had enveloped us with so much peace and assured us that Angela was safely home with Him. Yet, there were times when rage stirred inside me toward the one who committed this savage crime against Angela and our family.

The week after Angela's murder, when I was thinking of him, I heard God speak, not in an audible voice, but to my spirit . . .

"There may be no one else praying for this man."

Surprised and angered, I responded out loud, "So?"

A panic came over me.

"God, you don't want *me* to pray for him? Please don't ask me to pray for this man!"

I waited. There was no answer. I knew that was exactly what He was asking of me. The agony of Angela being dead, and dying in such a brutal way, seemed more than I could bear. The very thought of praying for Angela's murderer was offensive, and seemed so unfair for God to expect this. I struggled, resisting the very thought of it.

In obedience, I dropped to my knees; my insides were being tied into knots. Hesitantly, I spoke, "God, I have no feelings of compassion for this man, but I pray in obedience to You, that You would cause him to know You as Savior and Lord of his life."

By the time I finished, my stomach was churning. Out of obedience to God, I continued to pray for him and also for the people who were involved in Angela's life at the time of her death, even though I felt physically ill each time I prayed.

With the funeral over, family and friends had returned to their homes. One afternoon I began sorting through the few possessions Angela had left. To my surprise, while going through her things, I discovered a book of poems she had written. I felt like I had found a treasure. In these poems, she expressed with great emotion her desires and the intense pain and turmoil she often felt during her teenage years. She signed each poem, *FREE BIRD*. I remembered the talk she and I had about writing a book together to share her story and how God would fulfill His promises. After her death, I knew it was no longer possible for us to write a book together. Now, I held in my hands her writings telling of what she experienced during those difficult years of her life. Maybe she and I *will* share her story together after all, I thought.

One evening, I went out on the front porch and stood staring into the sky. How could it be possible that Angela was nowhere to be found? There wasn't a place on this earth where I could call her on the phone and talk to her. I yearned to see her, and to hold her, and to hear her voice. I had listened to old tapes on my answering machine hoping to find an earlier message with her voice still on it, but there was none. I thought of those messages I had so routinely erased before. I wanted to find something left of her life that I could hold onto. How could it be that I could never talk with her or hold her again? It was incomprehensible that she could be so full of life just days before, and now she didn't exist.

"She's gone," I spoke quietly to the darkening sky.

I thought of Angela's most recent phone calls. I remembered how she started asking me with each of her phone calls, "Mom, are you praying for me?" The anxiety in her voice always diminished when I reassured her of my prayers.

I closed my eyes, while my mind filled with memories. "God, I did pray for her."

A thought dashed across my mind. The gentle words of God spoke to me, *"Get your notebook, and read what I gave you at the women's retreat."*

The notebook! I had forgotten about it. The speaker at our women's retreat had spoken words of prophecy to me about Angela. I remembered writing them down. I ran into the house and up the stairs searching my room until I found the book. Eagerly, I flipped through the pages. There it was. My eyes focused on the words I had written only two and a half weeks before Angela's death.

'Remember the promises . . .

You are to be released from any guilt . . .

The prodigal will come home.'

I sat on the bed, astounded. Slowly, I re-read the words. *God! You told me two and a half weeks before she died that she was going home to be with You.* I thought she would be coming home to us. I had set the notebook aside and had even forgotten about it, being content and confident to wait for Angela to return home, willing to start a new life for herself. *The promise You gave me of restoration for Angela has been fulfilled! And all the guilt I've felt, all the questions I've wrestled with . . . Did I not do enough for her? Did she know I loved her? You knew how I would struggle.* I sat there taking it all in. *You are so real . . . so faithful. You did have the final victory in Angela's life and she is with You now.*

This was just the beginning of ways God poured out His grace and love. That week, I phoned Dotty, a close friend from our previous neighborhood to thank her for a picture she and the neighbors had given me the day of the funeral. It is a beautiful picture of Jesus tenderly holding a little lamb. His pierced, blood-stained hand gently held a helpless little lamb close to His bosom. The lamb nuzzled his tiny head into Jesus' strong shoulder. Its face was one of ultimate peace and pure contentment as it soaked up Jesus' love. It revealed a hint of a smile as it rested without reservation in Jesus' arms.

I studied this little lamb's face. I thought of the picture the Lord gave me of Angela dying in His arms, oblivious to any pain as she rested in His protective arms. The day of the viewing, her face was so like this little lamb; a restful peace, with the same hint of a smile also on her face. Dotty hadn't seen Angela before the funeral or known of the picture God had given me of Him holding her as she lay dying. I set the picture down. A handwritten note was on the back. It read, "This little lamb is Angela in the arms of Jesus."

I dialed her number, eager to let her know how much this picture meant to me.

Before I had a chance to thank her, she interrupted me, "Carol, there's a story behind that picture. When I was in the Christian bookstore I saw the picture on the wall. God spoke to me and said, *'I want you to buy that picture for Carol and Keith'*. I wanted to buy it for you, but I didn't have a lot of money to last for the rest of the week."

She laughed. "Can you believe I argued with God and told Him I couldn't afford it? After wandering around the store a few more minutes, I started to leave and He spoke to me again,

'I want you to buy that picture for Carol and Keith'. Without a doubt I knew God was telling me that you were supposed to have that picture, and I wasn't to leave the store without it. When I returned home, the neighbors said they wanted to get you something, so we put in together for it. Carol, I bought the picture, but I want you to know that God wanted you to have it."

Thank You God for yet another confirmation that what You revealed to me the day we viewed Angela is truth.

The following week, there were more miracles. Each day I received two to three phone calls from friends exhilarated and anxious to tell me how Angela's life and death, and the funeral service, had made an impact on their lives.

My friend Kathy called, "Carol, you know my daughter Laura and I have struggled in our relationship for years."

Kathy had suffered through an ugly, unwanted divorce and Laura blamed her for it. For years, she had held an attitude of bitterness against her mother. Laura knew Angela well, and Angela's death had deeply upset her.

"When we left your house on Saturday after the funeral, for the first time in years, Laura and I were able to talk. We cried together. We shared the hurt we've both felt for so many years. Carol, the healing that took place was nothing short of a miracle."

Shelly, a high school friend of Angela's called, "I needed to let you know how much your letter to Angela that you had read at the funeral meant to me. For a long time, my mom and I have had difficulty in our relationship. I made a decision on Saturday that our relationship is going to be better from now on."

My niece Lisa and her husband had buried their newborn infant son a few weeks before Angela's death. Lisa wrote to me in a card, "Aunt Carol, thank you for having your letter to

Angela read at the funeral. It really helped me with a lot of my feelings with Ryan, and in many parts I felt like I was writing it to Ryan."

I called Grandma Hunt at the nursing home, hoping to comfort her. She was hurting and needed to hear all that had happened. I didn't expect to hear Grandma so calm.

"Carol, I already know that Angela is with God. We had a luncheon this week at the nursing home and several young people from a small neighborhood school came to sing for us. I didn't want to go, but the nurse insisted it would be good for me. She wheeled me downstairs to the only vacant seat left at the table. A young girl sat next to me. She said hello and acted as if she knew me well. She said to me, 'I'm glad you came. I thought I was going to miss you.' Then she handed me a wooden cross that she said she had made just for me. When I held that cross in my hands somehow I knew that God was speaking to me through this little girl's gift. I knew Angela was with Him. After the performance the girl got up quickly and left before I had a chance to say anything else to her. I asked the other people at my table if anyone had told this girl about Angela's death. No one had. The next day, the nun who worked at the school came to visit. I asked her to find that little girl because I wanted to thank her. She called me back later and said, 'I can't find her. I don't know who she was or what happened to her.'"

I was amazed. It was as if God had lifted a veil and was allowing us see things in the spiritual realm that we don't always see.

There were people who accepted Jesus as their Lord and Savior. There were teenagers willing to get help for their drug and alcohol problems, as a direct result of Angela's life and death.

Seeing people's lives affected in such a profound way brought comfort to us and even joy in the midst of our tremendous pain. Each night, Keith returned home from work and expectantly asked, "Who called today?" And each day for at least a week after the funeral I was able to tell him of the newest miracle.

Shawn asked me one evening, "Did you notice the birds flying over the chapel the day of the funeral?"

Yes, I had remembered looking up before I entered the chapel, seeing hundreds of birds flying over and around the area. A friend had mentioned to me just a few days before how difficult it had been for her to concentrate during the funeral service because of the many birds flying and singing outside the windows of the chapel.

Shawn continued, "When we left the chapel to drive to the grave site, I realized I forgot my Bible. I hurried back to the chapel. It had been only a few minutes since we had left. Carol, there were no birds left! I walked inside and other people were in there preparing for the next funeral service. The presence of God and the peace that we so strongly felt in that room just minutes before was gone."

Maybe it wasn't a coincidence that so many birds had surrounded the chapel from the beginning to the end of Angela's funeral service. Maybe this truly was one more way God was showing me and our family that Angela, who so desperately wanted to be a *'Free Bird,'* was now free in the arms of her Savior.

The last entry in Angela's 'Book of Poems':

Baby, don't you cry,
Don't cry anymore.
One of these lonely nights,

Farewell, My Free Bird

You'll rise up and spread your wings,
And take to the sky.
Until the morning,
Baby, wipe your eyes.
                    Angela, FREE BIRD

Chapter Eighteen

REACHING OUT TOGETHER

"Let them sacrifice thank offerings and tell of His works with songs of joy." (Psalm 107:22)

In the months following Angela's death, there were many difficult moments that reminded us of our loss. That first Christmas without Angela was especially hard, but it was more important than ever for us to celebrate as a family. As I decorated the Christmas tree, I thought about Christmas the year before. It was the first time in many years our family had been together since Carl had joined the Marines. Carl had been on military leave and Angela had come home to recover from a drug overdose. Of course, none of us realized at the time that only four months later, Angela would be dead.

My recent trips to the mall reminded me of Angela. I saw several mothers and daughters shopping together, and in every store I saw displays of clothing that were Angela's favorite style. I felt a tremendous void inside, not being able to buy a gift for Angela.

One morning as I listened to the radio, I heard a man named Chuck Colson being interviewed by James Dobson, head of Focus on The Family radio program. They were discussing the Angel Tree Project that was sponsored by the Prison Fellowship program that Chuck Colson headed up. He spoke of children with incarcerated parents that would not be receiving a gift from their parent this year. He asked for donations of gifts that would be sent to these children so they could have a gift under their tree on Christmas morning.

I became interested and lost myself in the joy of shopping for the perfect gift. I found a beautiful sweater I knew Angela would like. I wrote a note expressing my love and wishes for a 'Happy and Blessed Christmas', then, as instructed, I wrote 'Older Teenage Girl' on the package before mailing it.

On Christmas morning as our family gathered by the tree and exchanged gifts with each other, I thought of another teenage girl opening her gift. I hoped she liked it. I felt a peace and a joy that made it easier for me to get through the rest of the day.

I learned that Chuck Colson had other prison ministries and needed volunteers to go into the prisons for seminars. The following February, I was one of many who attended an information meeting. I filled out an application. I wanted to be a part of their ministry, but I wasn't sure if I was ready to do this. It had only been months since Angela's murder, and so often I would suddenly be overcome with intense grief and sadness that left me physically and emotionally drained for days. I prayed that God would show me if I was to be involved in this ministry at this time.

I didn't hear from them for weeks, so I assumed I had not been chosen as a part of their seminars. Then one afternoon, I received a phone call that gave me my answer.

"Would you be interested in being a part of our next in-prison seminar?"

"What are the dates for this seminar?" I asked.

"April 8th, 9th, and 10th."

I tried not to show my excitement. "Yes, I would be interested!"

When he hung up, I couldn't contain myself. All alone in the kitchen I shouted with joy.

April 8th was Angela's birthday. I had been dreading the month of April since it was not only Angela's birthday but the anniversary month of her death.

I knew where I was supposed to be on her birthday.

I attended the required training with my family's blessing and with prayers and emotional support from friends.

On April 8th, I left home and followed the directions I was given to the Chino Women's Prison. I drove off the main highway and saw the prison at a distance. There were several large brick buildings all in a row and a tall chain link fence surrounding the large piece of property. I turned into the parking lot. Angela would have been twenty today.

I prayed that God would use me to reach out to someone. It would be like Angela and me reaching out together. The Angela I knew, without the addictions, loved to help people and make them happy.

I noticed the other volunteers arriving. "Here goes," I thought, as I headed for the brick building. Before we were allowed to go through the first of four locked doors, we had to present our identification, pass through the metal detector, and have our purses checked. As the last door slammed and locked behind us, I looked back to see the razor wire that surrounded the entire building. Guards were everywhere throughout the yard.

To my surprise, it looked like a college campus. The buildings were separated by rows of sidewalks and sections of lush green grass. Some women were leisurely sitting on picnic tables. Others were working. Most of them watched as all twenty-four volunteers followed the chaplain to the building where we would have our meetings.

We were forewarned about the blatant lesbianism to which we would be exposed. Yet, we were totally unprepared for what we saw.

One of the volunteers said to another, "I thought this was only a women's prison."

"It *is* only a women's prison," she answered.

"You're kidding!" she replied in disbelief.

It was hard not to take a second look or stare. Our minds played tricks on us as we tried to imagine that some of these women with male-looking bodies, manly haircuts and clothes were really women. Their hardened facial features and even their masculine gait, disguised their true sexual identity.

The prisoners' attendance at this weekend seminar was voluntary. I wondered what their response to us would be. Would they consider us intruders and resent us being here? We approached the chapel and we heard the beautiful voices of women prisoners singing praise to God. I was totally unprepared for the warm reception we received. When we walked through the door, we were surrounded by women hugging us and thanking us for coming.

The room was packed with over a hundred women of different races and nationalities, even the clothing was diversified. Some wore pant suits or dresses. Others wore the standard prison-issued outfit of jeans and a grey sweatshirt. Although there were a few inmates who stood at the back of the room eyeing us with suspicion, most of the women's faces reflected their joy at our arrival. Basically, this was the small, but strong core group of Christian inmates I had heard about. I realized with anticipation that this weekend was going to be a good experience.

Our *'Thriving and Surviving in Prison'* seminar began. The focus of the seminar was to help the women grow in their Christian life and to deal with problems of bitterness and loneliness, while learning the benefits of submission under proper authority. After each lecture, we broke into small groups, encouraging the inmates to apply the truths of Scripture, as we gave them the opportunity to share the hurts, defeats and victories they experienced in prison.

Several of the women shared their excitement and fears about their upcoming release dates. They knew the facts. Most inmates make it on the outside for only a short period of time. Many of their friends had been released, vowing never to come back, only to return to prison again in a short time. I saw the quiet desperation in their eyes as they talked about it.

A woman in her twenties started crying, "I don't want to take drugs anymore. I pray every day that I will make the right choices when I get out of here." Her voice shook and tears streamed down her face, "I want to be a good mom to my kids. I really want to make it this time."

I looked around our little circle of women and saw the tears in each of their eyes. They understood.

I thought of another place in time when a similar conversation had taken place when Angela and I had sat in juvenile hall together.

"Mom, when I get out this time I promise you it will be different. I'm going to make it, and someday, I want to help other teenagers who are going through what I'm going through now."

There were so many times Angela had a sincere desire to break free. But she didn't make the right choices. A few weeks after being released, she kept returning to her friends who were not really her friends and to a lifestyle that was self-destructive.

She was as sincere as these women sitting in front of me. They knew they were dealing with a powerful force.

As the weekend progressed, the volunteers became close with the women in our group. I was beginning to see that the benefits of this weekend were just as much for me as it was for these women. One afternoon while sitting in our tight little circle, an inmate shared her heartbreaking story. Her two young daughters had been murdered by her ex-husband, the father of the children. Her face was filled with grief as she spoke of the murder of her two little girls and the intense hatred and resentment she had felt toward her ex-husband. But, because of experiencing God's grace in her own life, she was now able to choose to forgive him, and, for the first time, she felt free to go on with her life. She was hopeful that this time she would make it on the outside.

As we sat in our circle, Marie, a very pretty young woman spoke, "Last time I left this prison, I was determined I'd never come back. I became a Christian while I was here. I knew the only way to make it on the outside was to find a church I could join. I knew I needed help. The first Sunday I was out of prison, I went to a church near my home. I was scared but I went anyway. After the service, no one even acknowledged me. I was disappointed, but I spoke to the pastor before I left."

Tears started falling as she continued.

"He was kind to me and asked me if I'd share my story from the pulpit the next Sunday. I agreed to do it."

People were handing Marie tissues, and a few of us sat close while putting our arms around her. It was all she could do to get the words out.

"It was so hard to stand up in front of the church and tell these strangers that I had just gotten out of prison and that I needed their help. After the service, I was ignored just as I had been the Sunday before."

Farewell, My Free Bird

The pastor apologized for his congregation, but it was too late. Marie had strongly felt the rejection. Before long, she returned to the streets.

"They don't want us in their nice little churches. But we can't make it out there without you stronger Christians to help us. We've tried everything else, and it doesn't work. We know God is our only hope."

Marie said, "To be honest, I'm having a hard time trusting you Christians again."

I knew that the response she received was not typical of all Christian churches; but unfortunately the one she attended did not extend to her the grace and compassion she so desperately needed.

The next morning, the volunteers dispersed themselves throughout the room to wait for the inmates to arrive. A tall, black lady came in. I recognized her. We had a brief conversation the night before. She sat next to me and started talking.

"I'm so happy since I found Jesus," she said. "You know, I'm not the same person I used to be. I've done a lot of wrong things, but now Jesus has freed me. I used to be a lesbian, but I have no desire for that now."

She stopped and looked at me wondering if it was safe to continue. Then she said, "And I've murdered someone. I've asked God to forgive me for that."

Time stood still for a moment, and my heart raced.

Lord, help me. I silently prayed.

Then I heard myself speak. "If you've sincerely asked God for forgiveness and invited Jesus to be Lord and Savior of your life, the Bible says you are forgiven, and yes, you are a child of God." My emotions were still going haywire inside, but this was the truth. I said a quiet prayer before I spoke again. Then, I told her briefly of Angela's murder.

"I pray that this man who murdered my daughter will be caught and convicted for his crime. But, God has done a miracle in my heart. After my daughter was murdered, God challenged me to forgive this man and to pray for his salvation. As hard as it was, I chose to forgive him, and I still pray for him. The same God who wants me to forgive and pray for my daughter's murderer is the same God who forgave you when you asked His forgiveness and became His child."

I don't know if she understood how hard it was for me to say that. I thought of how difficult it had been to obey God's prompting to forgive and to pray for this man's salvation. However, with time I've realized that by my obedience to God, by praying that Angela's murderer be set free from the chains that bind him, God was also loosing the chains of bitterness and resentment that so easily could have bound my heart.

The last night of the seminar had been set aside for the inmates to share. Most of the women expressed how grateful they were that we from the outside world had come to the prison to be there for them. One girl stood to say that she did not consider so much that she had been arrested, but that she had been rescued. "If God had not taken me off the streets when He did and allowed me to be put in jail, I wouldn't know Him like I know Him now." Her face couldn't have been more radiant. As I watched her and I observed her countenance, God processed something very special through my mind. *"This is like your Angela. If she could speak to you, she would say . . . 'Mom, if God had not taken me off the streets and allowed me to go home, I would never know Jesus like I know Him now.'"*

God's peace filled me as I stood there. The service ended with singing. I watched the volunteers and prisoners raising their hands together in worship. The woman who had murdered was lost in the joy of worship. In another corner of the room, I saw a girl who had been caught up in lesbianism being prayed over. Tears were streaming down her face, and before my very eyes I saw her face miraculously soften. These women knew first-hand what God's grace is all about. I had never been to a worship service as powerful as this one. I had never spent a more meaningful weekend as this one.

After loving and tearful goodbyes were said, I left the prison elated. As I walked to my car, I felt very close to Angela. On her birthday, we had truly reached out together.

Chapter Nineteen

MIRACLES AND REVELATIONS

"See to it that no one misses the grace of God and that no bitter root grows up to cause trouble and defile many." (Hebrews 12:15)

I continued asking God to help me through the process of forgiveness for this man who murdered Angela. Each time I prayed for him, I felt that same pit in my stomach. However, I knew it was the right thing to do, and I realized how important it was that I not allow bitterness to steal any of the joy that God had given me as He worked His many miracles in my life and in our family.

One day, God spoke to me again about Angela's murderer.

"He's just like your Angela."

I was horrified. Then I was given a picture of Satan with puppet strings controlling Angela, and just as he was controlling Angela in her strongholds and addictions, Satan was also controlling this man. I started to understand. Yes, this man murdered Angela, but behind it all was the ultimate enemy, Satan, who ripped us off.

First I felt anger, and then excitement. With confidence, I spoke aloud. "Satan, you did *not* have the victory with Angela, and because you dared to touch a child of God you're going to lose everything. You're going to lose the people involved in her life at the time of her death, and you are *even going to lose her murderer.*"

Satan would have no victory, but only defeat. Since God had asked me to pray for Angela's murderer, I knew there was hope that this man would respond to God. I pictured Satan hanging his head, wishing he had never touched her.

I began to pray more intently with purpose and fervency for this man and for the people who were involved in Angela's life just before her death. I prayed for each of them to be free from the bondage of drugs, crime, and prostitution, and that they would experience the reality of God's love and forgiveness. I claimed complete victory over the enemy, and I expected to see it happen. I asked God to continue to redeem Angela's life and death, and what the enemy intended for evil that God would turn around for good, even for the saving of many lives. I started praying the verses in Psalm 107 for them that God had given me for Angela.

It was on April 27, 1988, exactly one year after Angela's murder, when I received a phone call from a Detective Kenney from the San Francisco Police Department.

"We have the man that murdered your daughter in our custody, and we now have enough evidence to proceed with a murder trial. He's been convicted in federal court for a series of weapon charges. Now that he's in prison, the witnesses are willing to come forward and testify."

The detective told us that Angela had been staying in an apartment with two other prostitutes who were much older than she. This man that murdered Angela was a part of their world. Angela, at the young age of nineteen, trying to prove

Farewell, My Free Bird

she was one of them, talked too much and said things she shouldn't. This man became concerned Angela would cause trouble for him, so he decided he needed to *"take her out."*

The detective said it was apparent to him from his investigation that Angela may have been somewhat street smart, but in many ways she was very naive.

"I don't think she realized who she was dealing with and how much danger she was in when she hooked up with these people." he said.

We were grateful for this miracle that there would be a trial. But what he told us next was difficult to hear.

"This man is a twice convicted murderer. He's 46 years old. He's had eleven prior felony convictions. He was released from prison and placed on parole just a few months before he murdered your daughter, Angela."

Fourteen long months later, Keith and I packed our suitcases and headed for San-Francisco to attend the preliminary trial. Our family and friends were praying for us. As we drove across the Bay Bridge that would take us into San Francisco, I imagined what Angela might have been feeling and thinking the night this man took her across this same bridge from Oakland to San Francisco and then drove her into the Lincoln Park Golf Course. I wondered if she knew then of his intent.

It was early evening when we arrived.

I told Keith, "I want to find the golf course before we check in at the motel."

"Why don't we wait until morning?" he asked.

"Keith, this is important to me."

I opened my purse and pulled out the newspaper clipping and the police report I had saved. My stomach turned as it always did when I looked at the black and white picture of Angela's covered body lying on the ground at the golf course.

Detectives were bending over Angela measuring the distance from her body to the road.

'The bloody body of a woman in her mid-twenties was found in a wooded area early yesterday near the 17th hole at Lincoln Park Golf Course, apparently shot to death.'

How many times had I read articles like this one, feeling a brief moment of sadness, and then casually turning the page and continuing on with my own busy life. But this article was about our daughter.

Trees lined the narrow road that led into the golf course. We parked and got out of the car. Frantically, I walked up and down the road ahead of Keith, trying to match the trees in the background to the newspaper picture. I took the police report and had Keith pace off the distance from the entrance to where they had found her.

Keith carefully measured his steps, than stopped. "According to the report this is about where they found Angela." He looked around. "This is the 17th hole."

It wasn't enough for me to be close.

"But these trees in the background aren't exactly the same as the picture."

"Carol, that picture was taken over three years ago. The police report is accurate. This has to be the right area."

"But is this the exact spot?"

"I don't know if it's the exact spot." he said.

Tears welled up. "I have to know where she died. I need to find the place where they found her."

I turned to look at the green rolling hills and the ocean. We stood in silence listening to the distant sounds of the ferry boats and the crashing sound of the waves. Angela had always loved the ocean.

Within minutes a dense fog rolled in and night literally fell. The ocean disappeared. The horns of the now unseen cargo ships sounded almost scary. I had never experienced such a change. Suddenly, this was an eerie place to be. A cold chill washed over me.

So, this was what it was like the night Angela was murdered. Oh God, how very alone she must have felt, how terrified. I thought of Angela's desperate screams echoing in the night as her murderer shot her and stabbed her. No one would hear. Now, her dad and I stood in this very place unable to save her. How long had she lain on the ground in agonizing pain before her life drained from her?

Then I remembered.

And, this was the place, God, that You met her when she cried out to You in her despair. You held her and comforted her and You took her home.

Keith interrupted my thoughts, "Carol, let's leave."

I wanted to stay longer, but Keith insisted we leave. He took me by the arm and led me back to the car.

"If you want to, we can come back tomorrow," he said.

We checked into our motel and laid our weary heads on the pillow, wondering what tomorrow would bring.

The next morning, we traveled downtown to the court building, locating the detective's office on the fourth floor. Detective Kenney greeted us and led us to the first floor to the courtroom where the trial was scheduled to take place. He introduced us to Al Giannini, who was the assistant district attorney assigned to our case.

For the first time, we saw the witnesses. These were the people who had been involved in Angela's life just before her death. They were not young like Angela, but they were adults in their thirties and forties.

Along with them, we were told to wait outside in the hall before we were allowed to go inside the courtroom. I felt awkward, and I sensed they did too. It meant so much to Keith and me that they were willing to testify. It took courage for them to be here and somehow Keith and I wanted to express our appreciation, but this didn't appear to be the appropriate time.

We were directed into the courtroom and found seats toward the front. At any moment they would bring in the man who murdered Angela. I held Keith's hand and spoke a silent prayer for strength. The door opened. I watched this man saunter into the courtroom with a smirk on his face. His black straggly hair hung around his neck. He noticed the familiar faces seated in the back of the courtroom, the people he knew would testify against him. Before taking his seat next to the public defender, he gave them an intimidating look of disapproval.

So, this was the man who had brutally murdered Angela. This was the man who had caused our family endless grief. I couldn't take my eyes off him. I felt so many mixed emotions as I watched his every move.

Before the trial even had a chance to start, the public defender requested a postponement and the judge granted it. The bailiff led the man out. We left the court room disappointed. The witnesses gathered in the hall a few feet from us. One of the ladies began crying. I walked over to her and put my arm on her shoulder.

She looked at me. Tears were streaming down her face, "I'm sorry about Angela."

We hugged each other. She introduced herself as Sharon. A few of the other women gathered around us, each expressing their sympathy and telling us they would do whatever they could to help.

In the next few months, we returned three different times to San Francisco before the preliminary trial ended. The judge declared there was enough evidence to charge this man with

Angela's murder. Now we would need to wait for the jury trial.

One of the most important things that came out of the preliminary trial was getting to know Sharon and Ginger. These were the ladies Angela had lived with in an apartment several months before she was killed. Since Angela's murder, Sharon had gotten into support groups and no longer lived in bondage to a life of prostitution and drugs. It meant a lot to me that Sharon now had a job and was excited about *'making it.'*

Several months later, Sharon called me at home.

She said, "I know you must struggle with guilt, not understanding why Angela chose the life that she did." Sharon continued, "Just before Angela was murdered, she told me something that she didn't want me to tell anyone else, but I think you need to know."

I listened intently.

"When Angela was twelve or thirteen years old and just starting to take drugs, one afternoon she walked to the park near your home. She met three guys there who she had never seen before. They offered her marijuana. She took it, and smoked a joint with them. Then, they turned on her, and the three of them raped her."

I was speechless. It was like a puzzle piece that flew into place that answered many of my questions. I was in the process of writing Angela's story when Sharon told me this. It was clear to me that it was at the age of twelve or thirteen that Angela's behavior abruptly changed from normal teenage rebellion to extreme and bizarre behavior. I had always wondered if Angela could have been a victim of sexual abuse. I had read books and recently attended a seminar which described some of the choices that victims of sexual abuse often make. Although not all victims make the same choices, Angela's behavior fit into many of the common patterns I read about and were described. Many victims turn to alcohol, and/or drugs, to diminish their pain. They often have an intense need to be in control of their lives, trying to protect themselves from being hurt again or from ever feeling powerless once again, like they felt when they were victimized. They are likely to feel great shame and view themselves as not worthy of success or love and do not see themselves as valuable human beings. This often gives birth to self-destructive choices which enhance feelings of low self-worth even more. Some victims feel the need to pretend that their life and their destructive choices are good, and will defend their poor choices, while being tormented by the agony and pain that they feel inside. This is what I saw in Angela.

I thanked God for this revelation, but as the days passed, I was also forced to work through added grief and intense anger that Angela had been violently assaulted and raped. I shed many tears and felt intense rage toward the men who had violated my little girl. I thought of the painful years, the numerous crises, the puzzling self-destructiveness and bizarre behavior that Angela had displayed. Those men were as guilty of killing Angela as the man who shot and stabbed her.

All those years Angela was hurt and angry inside, and I didn't know why. Why didn't she tell me? Which day was it that she returned home wounded, her childhood stolen from her? Had I been too busy to notice that something was so terribly wrong? How destroyed and confused and alone she must have felt.

I wondered if she blamed me for not knowing. I knew when she didn't clean her room. I knew when she didn't do her homework. I knew almost everything, but I didn't know this.

Could this be why she showed such intense anger toward me? The one closest to her didn't understand or even suspect that something that devastating had happened to her. No wonder our communication had broken down. It made sense to me now why it had been so difficult for us to have a close relationship, even though we both yearned for it and had expressed that desire to each other.

I wished I could have said to Angela, "If only you had told me, I would have held you in my arms and cried with you. I would have done everything I could to protect you from further harm."

Had Angela thought the rape was her fault because she accepted drugs from them? Did she think we would have blamed her for what had happened? Had they threatened her or our family if she told? Oh God, to carry that weight alone was too much to bear for a little girl!

Again, I was comforted by a gentle reminder. *"Carol, she's not suffering anymore. She's free now."*

Thank you for Your victory, God. And until that wonderful day when Angela and I can be together again, hold her close in Your arms. Tell her that I love her and tell her that I'm sorry I didn't know.

CHAPTER TWENTY

HEALING FOR THE FAMILY JUSTICE FOR ANGELA

"I am confident of this: I will see the goodness of the LORD in the land of the living. Wait for the LORD; be strong and take heart and wait for the LORD." (Psalm 27:13-14)

1991 . . . . So much had happened in our family since Angela's death four and a half years ago. Carl had extended his military stay for another two years. He had been in Okinawa, and was then discharged from Camp Pendleton, in California, in 1990.

He felt deeply about Angela's death, but tried his best to keep his emotions under control, and continue on with his life. Although he stayed true to his faith in God, Angela's murder had caused him to question many of the things he once believed.

We thought Jason was handling Angela's death as well as could be expected, but we were wrong. One day our pastor Shawn believed God had spoken to him and told him that Jason was thinking about taking his own life. Shawn was shocked at the idea, because Jason seemed to be doing so well.

But he sat down with him one afternoon and hesitantly asked him, "Jason, are you having thoughts of suicide?"

Jason was stunned. "How did you know?"

Shawn explained and asked Jason further questions. He discovered that Jason had definite plans to take his own life. We were shocked! We were also amazed and thankful that God had revealed this to us. Jason was able to get the help he needed which involved counseling and a hospital stay.

Travis struggled with strong feelings of grief and anger. Even before Angela's death, Travis felt that he had lost his best friend when Angela left home for her life of drugs and prostitution. He recalled the good memories he had when they were growing up, sharing their secrets and doing fun and sometimes mischievous things together. Then, when she was murdered, he was also left with a heavy burden of guilt. Since Angela had told Travis before she left to return to Oakland that she may be in trouble, he felt, as her brother, that he should have protected her and kept her from returning. Even though we all knew no one could stop Angela when she was determined to do something, he wrestled for years with the guilt he felt. It was only recently that he found freedom from the tremendous guilt that had tormented him for years.

Travis enlisted in the Army and was a Scout in the 24th Infantry Division. His unit led the way into the invasion of Iraq against the Republican Guard during Desert Storm.

Fear gripped my heart as I continually listened to news of the war. So many times when the phone rang, I would wonder if this was another call that would shatter our world.

Fortunately, that first Gulf war did not last as long as everyone had anticipated, and after several months in Iraq, Travis returned to the United States and was stationed in Fort

Stewart near Savannah, Georgia. We immediately made plans to visit him. What a relief it was to be with him, thankful that he had survived the war! Travis and Keith weren't aware, but throughout the few days we were visiting Travis, there were several times I almost lost it emotionally. I was sure if I started crying, I wouldn't be able to stop, so I tried to spare Keith and Travis from the awkwardness of it all.

After Angela's death, Keith tried to be strong for the boys and me. I encouraged him to share his emotions; yet, whenever I felt immense waves of grief overpower me, I would try to be strong for my sons by holding back my tears, or I would find a private place to pour out my emotions. I was trying to spare my sons; trying not to cause them more pain. We were all hurting and grieving our loss. It might have been the best thing for us all to cry together.

God's faithfulness to our family was evident. And now, with His grace and His much needed strength, in October of 1991, Keith and I left for the murder trial.

We packed the car to travel the 400 miles to San Francisco. Since the preliminary trial, there had been so many delays and judicial postponements.

We received good news from Detective Kenney when we arrived. They had made contact with a witness whom, until now, they had been unable to locate. This witness was willing to testify at the trial. Many of our friends and family had been praying that he would be found. His testimony was critical.

Detective Kenney told us, "This is highly unusual. This guy is a hardened criminal. When he heard that we were looking for him, he showed up at the courthouse to collect his subpoena! We're all set now and ready to go forward with the trial."

The next morning, Keith and I sat waiting in an almost empty courtroom for jury selection to begin. The door opened behind us and a panel of over ninety people filled the room.

We sat in the courtroom surrounded by strangers. Unexpectedly, I felt overwhelmed by the harsh reality of Angela's death and by the realization that this was all taking place because Angela was murdered.

When everyone was seated, the judge stated that this case was about the killing of Angela Noe, a human being.

My heart skipped a beat when I heard Angela's name being read publicly and being referred to so impersonally. The people around us responded with gasps and hushed whisperings.

The agonizingly long process of questioning the possible jurors began. Many did not want to serve. Keith and I found ourselves on an emotional roller coaster watching those whom we thought would be good for the case, asking to be excused for personal reasons. A second panel of ninety people was brought in. It took two more days before a jury of twelve and four alternates was selected.

The trial began the following Monday morning. Each day was painful and draining as we listened to the detailed testimonies.

Earlier, a friend had asked, "Why are you and Keith putting yourselves through this?"

We knew it would be difficult, but we needed to know everything that had happened to Angela. We felt it was essential for us to be present *for* Angela in the courtroom, representing her, showing that she was a valuable, loved, and important person.

The most difficult witness to hear from was the coroner. He wheeled in a life-sized female dummy with red and blue dots strategically placed to identify every gun shot and stab wound on Angela. For hours he recounted appalling details, occasionally referring to the pictures of Angela on the board, pictures of Angela found murdered at the golf course, and pictures of her naked body on the coroner's table when they did the autopsy. Keith and I were barely making it through his testimony. He gave testimony of the six gunshot wounds on her body, none of which was the fatal wound. She had five stab wounds. Many of them were defense wounds from fighting off her attacker. The fatal wound was the stab wound to her heart. Keith swore under his breath in outrage. When the coroner told of the depth of Angela's stab wounds and the obvious struggle that had taken place, I saw Keith's clenched fist through my tears that I was trying so hard to hold back.

I remembered hearing of a lady who had been present at the trial for her son's murderer. She had quietly cried during a testimony and at the public defender's request, the judge ordered her from the courtroom saying her emotional state was influencing the jury.

I couldn't risk that happening. I sat in my seat wiping tears, aware of occasional stares from members of the jury, using every ounce of energy I had to stay in control and not make a scene. Finally, the coroner's testimony was over. I hurried to the restroom, finding an empty stall. There, I sobbed for my daughter and the horrors she suffered. Each day became more intense. Keith and I often left the courtroom at the end of the day feeling bruised and defeated, but God's grace continued to minister to us.

In the last few years, Keith and I had been praying together for this man who murdered Angela. We chose to obey God, and He worked His miracle of forgiveness in our hearts. We learned that forgiveness did *not* mean that what this man did was right, or that we no longer felt anger over what was done to Angela, or that we no longer felt tremendous pain, sometimes unbearable pain, over the brutal way Angela died. It did *not* mean that this man shouldn't have to pay for his crime against Angela and our family. Keith and I prayed for his conviction, just as much as we prayed for his salvation. The miracle for us was that we could go through this horrendous trial without revenge and hatred consuming us. For that, we are thankful.

One afternoon after a long and drawn out day in the courtroom, we headed back to our hotel. Across the street from the hotel, I noticed a young teenage girl sitting on the street corner. Her thin black coat was wrapped tightly around her. Her hair was blond and hung around her thin face.

As we parked the car in front of the hotel, I said, "Keith, I think that young girl is prostituting herself." I felt strongly that I was supposed to go and speak with her. I told Keith what I wanted to do and asked him to wait in front of the hotel, thinking it would be less intimidating for her if I went alone.

I started toward her only to see a man, probably her pimp, crouched behind a pole communicating with her. I walked toward her, wondering what I would do or say. She turned in surprise when I sat down next to her. "Is it alright if I sit down next to you?" I asked.

"This is my base you're on, lady." She looked over at her pimp who was now busy conversing with another man.

"What do you want?" she asked, obviously irritated at me.

"I just want to talk with you for a moment."

She nodded to the men driving by in their cars. She made eye contact with one man who had stopped at the light. I saw his embarrassment. He shook his head no and stared at me.

She responded, "Oh shit!"

She stood and watched his car turn the corner and disappear. She turned angrily toward me, and then rushed over to her pimp.

"Johnny!" she hollered and whispered to him.

He came to me, "What do you want?"

I shrugged my shoulders, smiled, and said, "Nothing in particular."

"Oh, ok," he answered and returned to the other man.

Farewell, My Free Bird

The young girl sat next to me again. Her blond hair covered her eyes. I could barely see her face.

"What 'ya want lady?"

"I just want you to know I'm praying for you."

"Praying for me? Why?"

"Because I see you're young and you're hurting."

"I'm not hurting," she said defensively. "I'm married. Hey, Johnny's my husband." Quickly, she got up again, yelling for Johnny. In hushed tones they spoke with each other. Then she moved closer to the street away from him and a few feet from me, trying to catch another male driver's attention.

Every few seconds she glanced in my direction. I knew she wouldn't come back and I knew if I stayed longer, I could get her in trouble with her pimp. I got up and walked back to the hotel. I prayed God would use my few inadequate words.

Keith asked what happened. When I began to tell him, I started crying. I felt a heaviness for this young girl. She was deceived, thinking she was worth no more than this, believing this was her destiny in life and maybe believing there was no way out for her. This young girl was all too familiar . . . Angela. Would this girl end up dead like our daughter someday? *Oh God help her, protect her. Show her the way out so she can live free!* I would never see her again, but I would never forget her.

The next morning we returned to the courtroom. It was mostly through the witnesses that God comforted us and gave us strength to sustain us through those very difficult days.

Sharon, Ginger, Frank, and Betty were the chief witnesses for the case. Each of them played a key part in the trial and their testimonies were important.

Frank, a man in his forties, had been a hired killer since the age of sixteen. He was there the night this man murdered

Angela. We trusted Detective Kenney, who believed Frank had no part in Angela's murder.

Throughout the testimony Angela's rebellious spirit was revealed. The public defender referred to her as the *'wild child'*. Sharon had referred to Angela as an out-of-control juvenile delinquent. Sharon said, "We had rules for our business, for our protection and safety, but Angela wouldn't follow them. We were afraid she was going to get us all into trouble."

Ginger cried on the stand, telling of her frustration toward Angela, "She just wouldn't listen to anyone."

Sharon told me later, "Angela would disappear for days at a time. When she would return, I'd confront her. She'd snap back at me and tell me I wasn't her mother, and I shouldn't be telling her what to do."

My heart broke when Sharon told me, "Angela drank or took drugs from the time she got up in the morning until she went to bed at night, or passed out, whichever came first."

We had lunch with the witnesses one afternoon. As we sat in the restaurant with Sharon, Ginger, Frank, and Betty, Frank shared of his determined efforts to live the *'straight life.'*

"I had my last shootout about a year ago," he said. "I decided the risks far outweighed the benefits. Besides, I'm getting too old for this," he said. He told us of the *'real'* job he had now.

Sharon and Ginger talked about their new jobs and the support groups they were now a part of. Ginger felt good about being enrolled in college. They referred to the years before going straight as wasted years.

Betty was the youngest, and probably in her thirties. She mostly listened and warmly responded to us. Most of them had been involved in drugs, prostitution and crime since they were teenagers. Each was at a different stage in life, but they were all doing better.

It was not a coincidence that all of them were coming out of such a life of bondage since Angela's death. We were witnessing a miraculous work of God!

The intense burden that weighed on us when we left the courtroom had lifted. In its place was an incredible joy. God's faithfulness and His love for these people were certainly evident. I thanked Him for working in their lives and permitting us to see His answer come to pass before our very eyes.

Keith and I returned to the courtroom hand in hand, with renewed strength and hope, confident that God had truly ordained this trial and the victory would be His.

All of the witnesses, except Ginger, were able to give their testimony in spite of the tremendous attacks from the public defender. When Ginger got on the stand, her fear of this man who murdered Angela overruled. She did not tell all that she knew. The district attorney referred to her as a hostile witness.

After two days of deliberation, the jury returned only to report that they could not agree on a verdict. Ten believed the man was guilty; two did not. It was a hung jury.

Al Giannini, the assistant district attorney, and Detective Kenney were discouraged. They had worked so hard to get a conviction.

Al Giannini told us, "Because the majority of jurors were in favor of conviction there's a chance we can request another trial. I'll do what I can."

We left the courthouse feeling weary and defeated. If God had miraculously allowed this trial, why didn't we get the guilty verdict we wanted? We didn't understand. It appeared that all had been lost.

Chapter Twenty-One

TO GOD BE THE GLORY

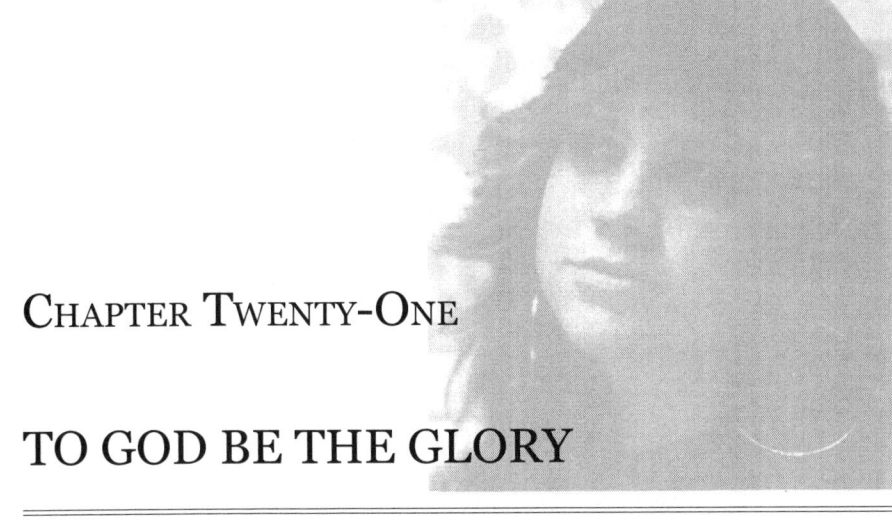

> *"Now to Him who is able to do immeasurably more than all we ask or imagine, according to His power that is at work within us, to Him be glory . . ."*
> *(Ephesians 3:20-21)*

A few months later, Al Giannini called us with good news. "Permission has been granted for a new trial!"

For the next fourteen months, every scheduled date we had for the trial was postponed, sometimes just days before the trial was to take place, usually postponed at the public defender's request. The witnesses would go through the uncomfortable and inconvenient task of meeting with the detective and have to review their testimonies from previous transcripts.

We were sure the public defender was counting on the witnesses becoming angry and discouraged and refusing to cooperate with the defense, or that with time, their memories of the case would fade.

In February of 1993, the new trial was scheduled to begin. We left for San Francisco, hoping this time the trial would take place. It would be six years in April since Angela's murder.

I was armed for the trial with the Scriptures God had given me in Isaiah 54 and other verses I had found in the Bible that referred to justice. One that I prayed often was from Isaiah 59 that spoke of God's displeasure when He looked and saw there was no justice. He was appalled that there was no one to intervene and that God Himself would work justice for the oppressed. Another was from Isaiah 61 that spoke of how much God loves justice.

Jewell, my special friend and Bible study teacher, called just before we left. "Carol, I was reading Ephesians 3:20-21 and the Lord told me these verses were for the trial:

> *'Now to Him who is able to do immeasurably more than all we ask or imagine, according to His power that is at work within us, to Him be glory . . .'"*

My prayer was that truth would be revealed in the courtroom, regardless of the public defender's schemes to twist the truth as he did so cleverly in the last trial. Most importantly, I prayed that God would be glorified in every way.

Before Keith and I left for San Francisco, I remembered two paperback books I had on my shelf in the den, entitled, *'Bible Promise Book.'* I felt prompted to bring them with me. I ran back upstairs, tossed them in my purse and hurried to the car.

This time the jury had been selected; the trial was scheduled to start in the afternoon. We drove directly to the courthouse, knowing we were running late and possibly missing the opening statements. We checked the courtroom first. It was locked and empty. We found Al Giannini in his office.

Farewell, My Free Bird

"I'm sorry," he said. "The public defender is sick and he went home. I've called two of the witnesses to be here in the morning. The public defender said he'd call me tonight at my home if he was not coming in tomorrow. So if you don't hear from me that will mean everything will be set to go in the morning."

We arrived the next day only to find out that the public defender did not call as he had agreed to and did not show up. There sat the two witnesses, Frank and Sharon, frustrated, discouraged and irate. Sharon had taken the day off work to be here. We were discouraged at the games the public defender was playing and getting away with. We wondered when this trial would begin.

Yet, it did give Keith and me the opportunity to spend time with Sharon. She was doing so well in her life. She spoke tenderly about Angela and told us how traumatic Angela's death had been for her.

As we talked, I told Sharon of the many ways God had revealed Himself to us as we dealt with the initial shock of Angela's murder and how we were surrounded by family and friends who came alongside us to comfort us and help us.

She listened as I told her how a few people from our church had been meeting in the mornings to pray. "The day after Angela was murdered, cars were lined up and down the street and the room was filled with people who came to pray for our family."

Sharon stopped me, "Because you were good people . . ."

"No. It was because they cared about us."

"Then, they didn't know about Angela's life, did they?"

"Yes, they knew about her life."

"My mother would never ever have told anyone in her church about me," she said. "Even now, I can't talk to my mother about those years of my life that I spent in prostitution and drugs." She looked at me with tears. "And I don't know why you would have anything to do with me, either."

I placed my hand on hers. "Sharon, I'm so proud of you. I'm proud of how far you've come and the progress you've made. We've experienced so much pain and trauma going through these trials, but the joy we have is the miracles we see in your life and in Ginger's life and the others."

We were both teary by this time. I so desperately wanted her to know how much joy, and how much comfort they brought us, and how precious and very dear she and the others had become to us. I valued each of them as a special gift from God.

Each murder trial was difficult, but this trial in particular proved to be the most intense of all. There were days we felt as if we had been on the front lines of a battlefield. Yet each day, God renewed our hope and filled us with His joy and strength as we watched Him do miracles in the trial and in the witnesses' lives.

We hadn't seen Ginger yet this time. Because of Ginger's previous testimony and her unwillingness to cooperate with the district attorney at the last trial, we didn't know how she would respond to us.

After a very difficult day in court, weary and discouraged, Keith and I were waiting for the elevator when we saw Ginger turn the corner. We all stood there for a few seconds uncertain of the other's response. Then, without hesitation, Ginger and I walked toward each other and embraced. Ginger told us about her new life and her new job. As we walked outside and down the court steps, Ginger told us of the apprehension she had felt all day while waiting to be called to the stand. When Betty, who had testified earlier in the afternoon, had returned to the victim witness room in tears, it made Ginger even more fearful.

Farewell, My Free Bird

Ginger said, "I was sitting in that room praying that God would give me courage to get on the stand and tell what I know."

Keith and I looked at each other in amazement when I suddenly remembered the *'Bible Promise Book.'*

"Ginger," I said as I pulled the book from my purse, "Take this and read the Scriptures in here on courage and fear."

We said goodbye, and on the way to the parking lot I squeezed Keith's hand in delight. We were amazed. We felt renewed and thanked God for His marvelous work in their lives.

The next morning, Keith and I sat in the victim witness room with Betty waiting for court to begin. The room was crowded, but we found a place at the table that was in the middle of the room. Ginger came in with a big smile. She had the *'Bible Promise Book'* in her hand. Even before she reached our table, she spoke loudly enough for everyone in the room to hear her.

"This is the neatest book!" She sat down across the table from us. "Just listen to these verses I found last night." She started reading verses that I recognized from Isaiah 54. "Tyranny will be far from you; you will have nothing to fear. Terror will be far removed; it will not come near you." She was beaming.

I sat in my chair, speechless. The verses that Ginger had read, the verses that had personally comforted her, were the same Scriptures God had comforted me with the day after Angela's funeral. I sat there in awe.

Betty sat next to me and by this time she was curious. "What is that book?" she asked.

Ginger proudly held it up to show her.

"Betty, I have one for you, too." I handed her the second book that had been in my purse.

Keith looked at his watch and motioned that it was time for us to return to the courtroom. As soon as we were out in the hallway, I poured out my excitement, "Keith, do you realize what the Lord just did?"

Once again, God was reminding me that this trial was taking place because of Him. We could rest in His power and victory.

Later that morning, during a break, I was walking down the hall and saw Detective Kenney bringing Betty to the courtroom. She was showing him her new book. They were unaware that I was approaching. I heard Betty say to the detective, " . . . and look at this!"

Respectfully, he bent his head to read what she was showing him, "Oh, that's nice," he replied politely.

When I returned to the courtroom, the jurors were in place. Minutes later, the judge entered and Betty was called to the stand. I noticed the murderer trying very hard to get Betty's attention, but she avoided looking in his direction. The public defender tried all his clever schemes to tear apart her testimony from the day before, berating her, trying to make the jury see Betty as the scum of the earth and incapable of telling the truth.

Poor Betty, what she had to go through! When the judge excused her and she got up to leave the stand, to my surprise, she was carrying her '*book*'. Innocently, she walked past the jurors with it in her hand. If any juror had been looking, they would have seen the bright bold letters on the front cover, '*Bible Promise Book.*' I realized she had no purse with her and had held the book in her hands while testifying.

I smiled. *I don't believe this, Lord. You are so good, and you really do have a sense of humor!* I thought of the Sword of the Spirit, which represents the Word of God. I asked that God

Farewell, My Free Bird

would continue to wield His Sword of Truth in this courtroom and that justice would prevail.

Detective Kenney invited us out to lunch that afternoon. He told us how different this trial was than other trials.

"Like Frank, for example," said Detective Kenney, "he came from a generation of crime where you don't snitch. But Frank told us that he's going to snitch on this guy, because he's done so much dirt to so many of us out on the street. Frank has never been on this side of the law. We don't even have an address or phone number for him. We send word out on the streets we're looking for Frank, and he shows up at the courthouse to collect his subpoena! It's unheard of!"

He continued, "We've subpoenaed these witnesses so many times. Usually what happens when you subpoena a witness more than once, they might show up, but they turn on the stand letting you know, *'I'm here, but I'm not cooperating.'* These witnesses keep coming back, and they seem to be getting stronger each time."

We listened with amazement, thanking God for His miracles.

"And," Detective Kenney added, "Their lives seem to be changing. Of course, we don't know what Ginger's going to do on the stand."

We knew how critical her testimony would be. Keith and I looked at each other remembering our conversation with Ginger the day before. "I think she'll do better this time," Keith said.

"We'll see," he said doubtful.

That afternoon, Ginger and I sat on the bench in the hallway waiting for her to be called to testify.

She confided in me, "Just talking about what happened makes me feel like I'm been pulled back into that life, and I don't want to be there again."

"Ginger, I want you to know I'll be praying for you." I assured her, "You're not going to be alone on that stand. God is going to be with you. I have a picture of you and Sharon. You both were in a pit. God brought you out, and He's the one who has set you on level ground. I'm praying you'll be able to glance back into that pit and tell the truth about what happened, but you're not going to teeter or fall back in."

Several times during her testimony, I saw her look at me needing those prayers. When the public defender cross-examined her it was intense and continued for hours. She surprised us all. Ginger did better than any witness had on the stand. I saw how painful it was for her, but she remained unbending and was not intimidated by the public defender's schemes. She held her own against his manipulation and attacks. When the public defender saw he was not succeeding in breaking her down, he took a picture of Angela from his desk and carried it over to the stand, setting it in front of Ginger.

"Do you know this girl?" he asked.

Ginger was weakening. Softly, she answered, her voice shaking, "Yes, I know her." He had Ginger identify her as Angela Noe.

Then he started in on her again. Continually, I prayed Scriptures over her asking God to sustain her. Within minutes, she bounced back regaining her confidence and boldness, telling the facts to the court.

Detective Kenney walked over to us and whispered, "I guess everybody has changed their life in this trial except me."

The public defender called his expert witnesses. He and the assistant district attorney presented their closing arguments. The judge instructed the jury and they went into the jury room for deliberation. All twelve jurors had to agree or this man would be found not guilty.

Al Giannini informed us, "If we get a guilty verdict it should take the jury at least a day and a half, probably longer, to review the evidence and make their decision."

A few hours later he entered the victim witness room where Keith and I were waiting.

He looked extremely nervous. "They have a verdict. I'll see you in the courtroom."

We were stunned. We knew what this probably meant. The walk down the hallway to the courtroom seemed twice as long as before. The courtroom was empty except for the bailiff and the court reporter. Soon, the courtroom started filling with people who had been involved in the case including Detective Kenney. Al Giannini paced back and forth while we waited for the judge to arrive. Everyone had to be in place before the jury could be called in.

The judge entered the courtroom, the jurors were called in.

The judge asked the jury, "Have you come to a decision?"

"Yes, your honor, we have," answered the jury foreman.

He handed the papers to the bailiff who carried them to the judge. Tension was mounting. The judge called Al Giannini and the public defender to the side bar. We watched intently as the three of them talked in hushed tones.

The public defender was smiling as he returned to his seat. I saw him pat this man on the leg. It looked like they were having their own victory party. My heart was racing and tension was mounting for all of us who were closely involved with this case.

The bailiff started to read . . . "The defendant is convicted of murder in the first degree."

Both Keith and I had been sitting on the edge of our seats. Keith fell back in his chair with relief. With relief and gratitude I whispered, "Thank You, Jesus!" I glanced over at the public defender and the convicted man. They were not as happy as they had been a moment earlier. The bailiff escorted Angela's murderer out of the courtroom.

The jury was dismissed. Most of the jurors looked straight ahead, avoiding any eye contact with us. But a few of them looked at us and returned my smile that I hoped conveyed my thankfulness to them.

There were hugs of joy. The room was filled with excitement and expressions of appreciation and relief. What a miracle! *To God Be the Glory!*

We returned home weary but exhilarated. The next night we celebrated with our sons and our church family. We ordered a cake and had written on it . . . *"To God Be the Glory!"* We sat in our living room telling of God's miracles. Wayne, our worship leader, played his guitar as we sang praises to God. There was so much joy and thanksgiving.

Four months after the conviction, we drove back to San Francisco for the sentencing. Sharon and Ginger were also present for the sentencing.

Before the judge gave his ruling, the family was given permission to speak. Keith spoke briefly of the devastation Angela's murder had brought on our family. I read a written statement telling of the tremendous pain our family experienced as a result of this man murdering Angela, what it was like to live my life without her. I pleaded with the court for this man to be sentenced to life **without** the possibility of parole so that other girls like Angela, and other families, would be spared from experiencing the devastation and suffering that we have experienced; asking the judge to keep this man in prison so he would never be allowed to kill again.

Jason had prepared a letter he wanted his dad to read that was intended for the judge and for this man who had murdered his sister. When I finished reading my letter, Keith stood and read Jason's letter in the courtroom.

"Life for me as a thirteen year old boy in junior high school was not very complex until the day I came home from school, and my mother received a devastating phone call. I knew that this call was different. I saw the shock and horror on my mother's face and the despair in her voice. When she hung up the phone, she told me that my sister, Angela, was dead. My sister had been murdered.

I'm not thirteen anymore, but I still live with the painful memories, and the deep loss of my sister. I never got the chance to say good-bye to Angela, or say I love you, Angela, before she died.

Unfortunately, I did not have the ability to deal with or understand my sister's murder. I plunged into severe depression and a rage so intense that I needed to be hospitalized. I wanted to take my own life. I didn't want to live anymore. After a month's stay in the hospital, I was found void of any suicidal threat to myself and released, but needed continual counseling to work through my grief and my anger.

I still don't know if I could ever forgive this faceless person who unnecessarily murdered my sister, whom I'll never be able to see or speak to again. I know God can forgive this man if he were to seek it. I want the murderer to know . . . you can have forgiveness from God if you really want it."
Jason Noe, Angela's brother

We couldn't tell how our statements affected this man, but to our relief when the judge spoke, he sentenced Angela's murderer to life without the possibility of parole.

This was a victory for us and for Al Giannini and Detective Kenney. They and so many others had worked so hard to get a conviction. Words could not express our appreciation for all they did to make this possible.

Before we left, I asked Al Giannini, "Is it really over?"

I knew that murder convictions are often overturned and that convicted murderers seldom serve their full sentence in prison.

He smiled as he reassured me, "We've got a life sentence without the possibility of parole. Yes, it's really over!"

We left San Francisco, and headed to our home in Los Angeles County, in Hacienda Heights. Finally, the trial was over. We felt joy and relief for the sentencing of Angela's murderer, but the pain of the loss of our only daughter would always remain in our hearts. God had continually covered us with His grace as we witnessed His miraculous intervention in the trial and in so many people's lives that were a part of this trial. But most of all, I was overwhelmed and thankful for His faithfulness in bringing Angela safely home with Him. Peace and comfort enveloped me as I was reminded that she wasn't suffering anymore, and that someday we would see each other again. What a great day that will be.

Angela, until that wonderful day comes . . . *Farewell, my Free Bird!*

EPILOGUE

Seven years later, we were surprised with another phone call from Al Giannini.

"I'm sorry to have to tell you this. The 9th U.S. Circuit Court of Appeals has overturned the murder conviction for your daughter's murderer because of claims by the defense that racial prejudice was shown during the trial."

We were in disbelief. What racial prejudice had been shown in the trial? In fact, there were numerous times Keith and I expressed concern that the judge went out of his way to cater to the public defender's demands and schemes to withhold the truth from the jurors and manipulate the trial.

"We have permission to have another trial," Al Giannini said. "We're hoping we can find the witnesses. But, even if we do find them, they may not be willing to testify again." he said. "I'll get back to you as soon as I know."

Miraculously, all the witnesses were found, and all were willing to return to court and testify. When the public defender realized there would be another trial and all the witnesses were willing to fully cooperate, he encouraged Angela's murderer to accept a plea bargain for second degree murder. This was the first time the murderer confessed to murdering Angela, and they agreed he would serve ten more years in prison for Angela's murder. We didn't realize his federal charges would be included in the plea bargain.

He is now out of prison and is on parole. He was released in January of 2010. We are very disappointed in the justice system and upset that a three-time convicted murderer could be released from prison. We continue to pray for his salvation and that he would choose to give his life to Jesus Christ, but we intently pray for the safety of the witnesses who risked their lives when they bravely came forward to testify.

God's miracle was not only the verdict that kept this man in prison for many years, but it was also the miraculous work He did, and continues to do, in the witnesses lives.

Through the years, we kept in contact with Sharon and Ginger. The year after Angela's murderer was sentenced, Sharon traveled from the San Francisco area to visit us in our home in Hacienda Heights. It was important to her that we visit Angela's gravesite. As she and I sat on the ground next to Angela's grave, reminiscing about Angela, Sharon also spoke of her new life free from prostitution and addictions. As we were getting ready to leave, she opened her purse and pulled out a token.

With great emotion she said, "This represents six years of my life being alcohol and drug free. I want Angela to have this." She lifted the vase that was set below the ground in front of Angela's gravestone. "Angela, this one's for you," she said, as she carefully placed her treasured token in the ground.

God has comforted our family with His many blessings and miracles. He has held us together through this tragedy that has brought us much pain and sorrow. He continues to be faithful to each one of us.

When God impressed upon me to begin writing Angela's story, I had many reservations about exposing my daughter's life to others. But, I knew the *real* Angela without the addictions cared about other people, and her heart's desire was that her life could make a difference. She would be pleased if she knew the story of her life could help just one person.

Angela's story would be just a sad story, if it wasn't for the faithfulness and blessings of God. God has used and continues to use Angela's life and death and what He did through it, to bring healing for others.

Angela's favorite cousin, David, recently wrote to me telling me of his thoughts and memories about Angela. "For me and my friends who had no parental obligations to her, she was simply a joy to be around most of the time, and one of the funniest people I've ever known."

David was also aware that there absolutely were two Angelas. He spoke of the Angela that was the troubled, rebellious girl who made bad choices and continually suffered the consequences, and then he spoke of the Angela who was the gregarious, fun-loving, ebullient, cheerful life of the party, who always loved to make people laugh and smile.

"Sometimes I think this second Angela is the one that often drove her to make bad choices. If something sounded fun, she would usually choose it regardless of the consequences," David said.

"Another thing you might find interesting," David added, "is that Angela believed she had her own little ministry of sharing Christ's message with people who weren't familiar with it, and many of those people she chose to hang with were not. She would get so happy when she felt that she had touched someone's life by doing so."

The difficult part for Keith and for me and our sons is that the Angela we all knew that loved people, that was fun and loved to laugh and make others happy, got lost in the darkness of the drug addictions and many of the choices she made began to control her. The revelation of Angela's molestation at such a young age made us understand that life must have become very complicated for Angela and surely caused her great pain and confusion.

I know that God's desire was to heal Angela and for her to experience His healing and freedom here on this earth, but sadly, we watched Angela choose her own way instead of God's way for her life. In John 10:10 it says . . . *"we have a real enemy that comes to kill, steal, and destroy, but God comes to give us life, and life abundant."* Sometimes I think how wonderful it could have been for Angela, and for our family, if she had chosen to trust God for her life and experience His love and healing from the pain and confusion she felt. But, I know she's experiencing that now. We will forever praise God that He was there for her when she cried out to Him and that her search for freedom ended in His arms. He took her from this life to eternal life, but we will forever miss her presence in our life.

As I finished writing this book, I re-read the last few verses in Psalm 107, that God gave me for Angela before she died . . . *"Let them give thanks to the LORD for His unfailing love and His wonderful deeds for men. Let them sacrifice thank offerings and tell of His works with songs of joy."*

Writing this book has been with the hope that God could use Angela's story to minister encouragement and hope to others who are going through their own struggles. And, it is my way of giving God thanks and telling Angela' story with songs of joy, giving Him the glory for the great things He has done!